Should I Refinance My Rental Property?

THE REAL ESTATE INVESTING
MENTOR

THE AFFORDABLE $50K COACHING ALTERNATIVE

James Orr
The Real Estate Financial Planner™

Published by:

Real Estate Financial Planner LLC
PO Box 2163
Loveland CO 80539

https://RealEstateFinancialPlanner.com

First edition November 2024.
File: 2024-11-02 - Should I Refi My Rental Property

This publication is designed to provide accurate and authoritative information regarding the subject matter covered. It is sold with the understanding that the publisher is not engaged in rendering legal, accounting or other professional advice or services. If legal advice or other expert advice is required, the services of a competent professional person should be sought.

From a *Declaration of Principles* jointly adopted by a Committee of American Bar Association and a Committee of Publishers and Associations.

This is a work of fiction. References to clients in this book are fictional and have been modified and changed from any possible real situations to protect the identities of clients and to simplify the stories for clarity. In some cases, significant parts of the stories have been changed. In some cases, stories have been completely fabricated to illustrate a concept. Any similarities to people alive or dead is purely coincidental.

AI Disclosure: While James Orr authored the original version of this content, AI was used extensively to draft, proofread, edit, improve and write subsequent versions and variations.

DEDICATION

Dedicated to my wife Tammy. I have no words.

FREE DOWNLOAD

The World's Greatest Real Estate Deal Analysis Spreadsheet™

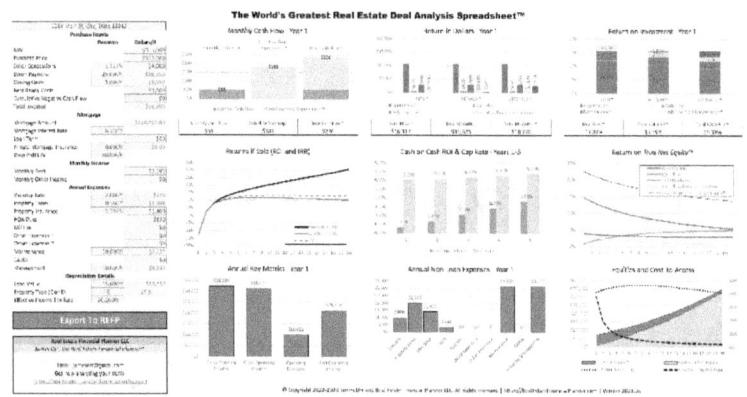

Thank you for purchasing this book and taking the next step toward mastering real estate investing.

As a special bonus, you can download *The World's Greatest Real Estate Deal Analysis Spreadsheet*™ for free. This powerful tool will help you analyze deals like a pro, ensuring you make informed, profitable decisions.

Download your free copy now and start running the numbers with confidence.

https://REFP.com/spreadsheet

Table of Contents

Should I Refinance My Rental Property?

Refinancing can be one of the most powerful financial tools in your real estate investment strategy—when you know how to use it effectively.

In this book, we're diving into what refinancing really means, the types of refinancing options available, and when it makes sense to consider refinancing your rental property. You'll learn about key metrics like return on equity, cash flow impact, and risk management strategies to help you make informed decisions.

We'll walk through different scenarios, from reducing your monthly payments to cashing out for new investments, and we'll explore both common and uncommon methods to analyze your potential returns before and after refinancing. Along the way, you'll gain a solid understanding of how refinancing can align with your goals for financial independence, liquidity, and portfolio growth.

While some calculations may overlap with decisions about selling a property, refinancing brings its own unique considerations. If you're interested in exploring those distinctions, you can find more detailed guidance in our companion book and spreadsheet, *Should I Sell My Rental Property?* Let's get started with the foundational knowledge you'll need to master refinancing as a strategic advantage in your investment journey.

What Does It Mean to Refinance?

Refinancing a rental property means replacing your existing mortgage with a new one, typically with different terms. The new loan pays off the balance on your current mortgage, and you begin repaying under the new terms. This can involve changing the interest rate, adjusting the length of the loan term, or even taking cash out if the property has built up significant equity.

The goal of refinancing is to optimize your financial position—whether by lowering monthly payments, freeing up cash for new investments, or managing debt more effectively within your real estate portfolio.

Why Refinancing Matters for Real Estate Investors

Refinancing is a powerful tool for real estate investors because it allows you to actively use your equity to improve returns rather than letting it sit passively in the property. Over time, your property's *return on equity* (ROE) tends to decrease, even as returns from appreciation, cash flow, debt paydown, and other areas grow in absolute dollar amounts.

Here's why ROE declines as your property matures. As you hold a property over many years, you pay down the loan, its value appreciates, and your equity grows. While this equity is beneficial, it doesn't always work as efficiently as it could.

By refinancing, you can unlock some of that equity to keep it working for you. Let's look at how different return factors grow over time and why they often lag behind the growth in equity.

- **Appreciation** - As your property appreciates, the dollar amount of appreciation tends to increase each year if we assume a consistent rate (such as 3%). This means the value of the appreciation grows over time. However, since your equity usually grows faster than the appreciation in dollar terms, the appreciation as a percentage of your total equity tends to drop.
- **Cash Flow** - Cash flow generally improves over time because rents tend to increase, while the mortgage payment stays fixed with a fixed-rate loan. Even if expenses like property taxes, insurance, and maintenance increase at the same rate as rents, your cash flow still tends to grow because rent is typically a larger number than these expenses. However, the rate at which cash flow improves is usually slower than the

rate at which your equity grows, which gradually reduces your ROE.

- **Debt Paydown** - As you continue to make mortgage payments, you pay down more principal each year, which helps increase your equity. While debt paydown grows in absolute dollar value, the percentage return on your growing equity from debt paydown declines over time.
- **Cash Flow from Depreciation™** - For 27.5 years, the IRS allows you to take a consistent depreciation deduction on residential rental properties, providing tax benefits that improve cash flow. Although this dollar amount remains fixed during that period, your equity in the property continues to grow, which means the return on equity (ROE) from depreciation gradually declines. After 27.5 years, the depreciation deduction goes to zero, causing this source of return to disappear entirely and further lowering your ROE.
- **Reserves** - If you hold a certain number of months' worth of reserves, this reserve amount may grow as expenses increase, but it rarely keeps pace with the property's equity growth. This slower growth in reserve requirements versus equity also means a shrinking ROE over time.

In the end, although returns from appreciation, cash flow, debt paydown, and reserves generally improve in dollar amounts over time—and depreciation remains fixed—these returns are typically outpaced by the property's growing equity. This results in a decreasing return on equity (ROE) over time. Refinancing can be a valuable strategy to access this idle equity and reinvest it in ways that keep your returns strong and efficient across your portfolio.

Types of Refinancing

There are two main types of refinancing for rental properties: rate-and-term and cash-out refinancing. Each serves different goals, so it's important to understand how each one works and when it might align with your investment strategy.

- **Rate-and-Term Refinance** - Also known as a limited cash-out refinance, a rate-and-term refinance is primarily aimed at obtaining better loan terms, such as a lower interest rate, a different loan duration, or removing mortgage insurance. You may also increase the loan balance slightly to cover closing costs or prepaid expenses, allowing you to refinance with minimal cash out of pocket. Additionally, you can receive a small amount of cash back—typically limited to the lesser of 2% of the new loan amount or $2,000, per lender guidelines. For example, if you're refinancing an existing balance of $200,000 and your closing costs are $5,000, you could add the $5,000 to your loan and receive up to $2,000 cash back, resulting in a total new loan amount of $207,000. This type of refinance is typically used when the goal is to improve cash flow or adjust the loan term without substantially increasing your loan balance.
- **Cash-Out Refinance** - A cash-out refinance allows you to access a portion of your property's equity by taking

out a new loan larger than your existing mortgage balance. The extra funds beyond your current mortgage can be used for various purposes, such as reinvesting in new properties, funding property improvements, or consolidating debt. With a cash-out refinance, you can increase your loan balance significantly, up to a maximum loan-to-value (LTV) ratio as allowed by the lender. Investors typically consider cash-out refinancing when they want to leverage their property's equity for additional investments or other strategic financial moves.

Choosing between these options depends on your goals: rate-and-term refinances are best for optimizing loan terms, while cash-out refinances provide access to equity for reinvestment or other financial uses.

Reasons to Consider Refinancing

There are many strategic reasons to refinance your rental property. Refinancing can help you strengthen cash flow, reduce risk, increase liquidity, and improve your portfolio's overall returns. Here are some key reasons why investors often choose to refinance:

- **Lowering Your Interest Rate** - Securing a lower interest rate can significantly reduce your loan costs over time and often improves cash flow, especially if it's a substantial rate reduction. Lower interest payments free up funds for reinvestment or reserves, which strengthens your overall financial position.

- **Reducing Monthly Payments** - Refinancing to a lower rate or extending the loan term can reduce your monthly mortgage payments. This can boost cash flow on the property and provide more funds for other investments or reserves, allowing for a more comfortable financial buffer.
- **Cash-Out for New Investments** - Cash-out refinancing lets you access equity in your property to fund new investment opportunities. Many investors use cash-out proceeds to buy additional properties, expanding their portfolios without using personal savings.
- **Shortening or Extending Loan Term** - Adjusting the loan term to a shorter period can help pay off the property sooner, reducing total interest costs. Alternatively, extending the term can lower monthly payments, improving cash flow if that's the primary goal.
- **Debt Consolidation and Credit Improvement** - Cash-out refinances can help you pay down higher-interest debts, which can improve your debt-to-income (DTI) ratio and credit score. This, in turn, could allow you to qualify for better financing terms on future property purchases.
- **Funding Property Improvements** - Cash-out refinancing can provide funds for property improvements or upgrades that may increase rental income or boost the property's value. Furnishing a

property to turn it into a short-term rental, for example, can often significantly improve cash flow.

- **Reducing Risk with Fixed vs. Adjustable Rates** - Refinancing from an adjustable-rate mortgage to a fixed-rate mortgage can provide stability by protecting you from potential interest rate hikes. Fixed-rate loans lock in your monthly payments, reducing uncertainty and helping you plan for the long term.
- **Increasing Cash Reserves and Liquidity** - Cash-out refinancing can also be used to increase cash reserves, which improves liquidity. Having more accessible funds reduces financial risk, providing a safety net for unexpected repairs, vacancies, or economic downturns.
- **Optimizing Return on Equity** - As equity grows, your return on equity (ROE) often decreases. Refinancing allows you to pull out some of that equity and reinvest it, which can lead to a higher overall return on your investment capital.
- **Achieving Financial Independence** - Refinancing can help you accelerate your journey to financial independence by unlocking capital to create additional income streams. You might use funds to pay off another rental property to improve cash flow, invest in stocks or bonds with a safe withdrawal rate, or purchase an annuity for steady income.
- **Supplementing Down Payments for Other Properties** - Cash-out refinancing can provide funds to cover down payments on other properties, helping you avoid private mortgage insurance (PMI) by reaching a 20% down payment. This allows you to expand your

portfolio without paying PMI, which improves your cash flow.

- **Buying Down Mortgage Rates on New Properties** - Cash-out refinancing can also fund rate buydowns on new property loans. Lower rates on these loans improve your cash flow across your portfolio and enhance your overall returns.
- **Generating Capital for Lending Opportunities** - Refinancing can free up capital to participate as a hard money lender or an investment partner in other real estate deals. This diversifies your income streams and can generate higher returns outside of direct ownership.
- **Freeing Up Loan Spots for New Purchases** - Sometimes, refinancing allows you to pay off a smaller mortgage on another property in full, freeing up a loan spot and enabling you to qualify for additional 30-year fixed-rate financing on new acquisitions.
- **Improving Asset Allocation** - Refinancing can be a way to shift funds from one asset class (like equity in rental properties) into another, such as stocks, bonds, or other investments. This can diversify your portfolio and improve its resilience to market changes.
- **Funding Marketing and Acquisition Costs** - Investors sometimes refinance to pull out cash to fund marketing efforts, down payments, and closing costs for creatively financed deals. Having accessible cash for these costs enables you to take advantage of more flexible financing structures in new acquisitions.
- **Supporting the BRRRR Strategy** - The BRRRR (Buy, Rehab, Rent, Refinance, Repeat) strategy relies on refinancing after a property has been improved to

recoup your investment. By refinancing, you can pull out the capital invested in the property's rehab and use it to fund your next BRRRR project, enabling you to expand your portfolio without additional cash injections.

Each of these reasons can add value to your investment strategy, but the best refinancing option depends on your specific goals, property performance, and long-term financial plan.

Common Refinance Limits

Refinancing a rental property comes with several limitations that vary by loan type, lender, and specific program guidelines. Here's a look at the most common refinance limits you'll encounter with both rate-and-term and cash-out refinancing.

- **Loan-to-Value (LTV) Limitations** - Lenders cap loan amounts based on maximum LTV ratios relative to your property's appraised value; for rate-and-term refinances on investment properties, the LTV limit is typically up to 75% for one-unit properties—including single-family homes and condos—and up to 70% for two- to four-unit properties; for cash-out refinances, the maximum LTV generally decreases to 70% for one-unit investment properties and down to 65% or 60% for two- to four-unit properties.
- **Credit Score Requirements** - Refinance loans generally have minimum credit score requirements, and the standards are often higher for investment properties compared to primary residences. For conventional

refinances, you'll typically need a minimum credit score of 620 for rate-and-term refinances, though some lenders may require scores of 680 or higher, especially for cash-out refinances. Higher scores may also allow for better terms and interest rates.

- **Seasoning Requirements** - Lenders often impose seasoning requirements, meaning you must own the property for a minimum period before refinancing. This can vary by lender, but six months is a common requirement for rate-and-term refinancing, while cash-out refinances may require you to own the property for 12 months or more. If the property was recently purchased, lenders may also look at whether it was acquired with cash or financing, as this can impact eligibility and terms.

- **Debt-to-Income (DTI) Ratios** - Some lenders evaluate your overall DTI ratio for rental property refinances, particularly for cash-out refinances. A lower DTI can increase your chances of approval and may impact loan terms.

- **Property Condition** - Lenders may require the property to meet certain condition standards, especially for cash-out refinances. Significant repairs or deferred maintenance may need to be addressed before refinancing.

- **Number of Financed Properties** - Many lenders limit the number of financed properties an investor can hold. Conventional loans often cap this at 10, which can restrict refinancing options if you already have multiple financed properties.

These limitations are designed to protect lenders by ensuring borrowers have the financial stability and equity to support the refinance loan.

Typical Costs Associated with Refinancing

Refinancing a property involves several typical costs, which can vary based on the loan type, lender, and property specifics. Here are the main costs you can expect:

- **Loan Origination Fees** - Fees charged by the lender for processing and underwriting the loan. This can range from 0.5% to 1% of the loan amount.
- **Appraisal Fees** - The cost of a professional property appraisal, which lenders require to determine the current market value. This typically ranges from $300 to $600.
- **Title Insurance and Title Search** - Fees for a title search to confirm clear ownership and for title insurance to protect the lender against claims on the property. These costs vary but can total $500 to $1,000.
- **Recording Fees** - Fees paid to the local government to record the new mortgage, usually costing around $50 to $250, depending on location.
- **Prepaid Interest** - Interest charged from the date of closing until the start of the first monthly payment, calculated based on your loan interest rate.
- **Property Taxes and Insurance Escrow** - Lenders may require an escrow account for property taxes and

homeowners insurance, collecting a few months' worth of payments upfront at closing.

Common and Uncommon Analysis

When considering a refinance on a rental property, two main types of analysis can help guide your decision:

- **Break-Even Point (Common Analysis)** - For a rate-and-term refinance, calculating the break-even point is essential. This analysis determines how long it will take for the savings from lower monthly payments to cover the refinance costs. Knowing your break-even point helps you assess whether the refinance makes financial sense based on your timeline for holding the property.
- **Change in Overall Return (Uncommon Analysis)** - For a cash-out refinance, it's valuable to analyze how pulling out equity impacts your overall return on investment (ROI). By calculating the expected returns on the new investment or use of funds, you can see if the increase in debt leads to higher total returns, helping you determine if the cash-out refinance aligns with your investment strategy.

Both of these analyses provide insight into the financial impact of refinancing and help you make a more informed decision.

Calculating Your Break-Even Point

Calculating the break-even point for a rate-and-term refinance is a straightforward way to determine if refinancing will enhance your rental property's cash flow over the long term.

The break-even point is essentially the time it takes for the savings from reduced monthly payments to offset the upfront costs of refinancing.

Here's how to calculate it:

1. **Calculate Total Refinancing Costs** - Add up all costs associated with refinancing, including loan origination fees, appraisal fees, title insurance, and other closing costs. This total represents your initial investment in the refinance.
2. **Determine Monthly Savings** - Compare your current monthly payment to the new monthly payment on the refinanced loan. The difference between these payments is your monthly savings. For example, if refinancing reduces your monthly payment from $1,500 to $1,350, your monthly savings is $150.
3. **Calculate the Break-Even Point** - Divide the total refinancing costs by your monthly savings to find the number of months required to break even. For example, if refinancing costs $5,000 and your monthly savings is $150, your break-even point is approximately 34 months (5,000 ÷ 150).

4. **Evaluate Against Your Timeline** - If your break-even point aligns with your intended timeline for holding the property, refinancing could make financial sense. However, if you plan to sell the property before reaching this point, you may not recover the costs, making refinancing less advantageous.

It's also helpful to compare the total interest cost of the new loan to your existing loan. Extending the loan term may lower your monthly payments but could increase the total interest paid over the loan's lifetime. This is an important consideration if you're more focused on reducing long-term interest costs than simply lowering monthly payments.

A break-even analysis offers a clear view of how long it will take to recover refinancing costs and whether the refinance supports your broader investment strategy.

Several online tools can help you quickly calculate the break-even point.

Common Rules of Thumb for Refis

Several rules of thumb can help you quickly assess if a refinance might be worth exploring. While these guidelines aren't strict, they offer a useful starting point:

- **Interest Rate Differential** - A common rule of thumb is to consider refinancing if the new interest rate is at least 0.5% to 1% lower than your current rate.

However, for larger loan balances, even a 0.25% rate reduction may be worthwhile, while smaller loans often need a larger drop to justify the costs.

- **Recouping Refinance Costs** - Many investors look for a break-even point within 24 to 36 months. This timeframe allows you to recoup the refinancing costs relatively quickly, ensuring that any savings afterward contribute directly to cash flow or reducing overall interest costs. If you plan to hold the property long-term, this break-even period is usually a solid indicator.
- **2% Rule** - Some investors apply a "2% rule" for refinancing, meaning the total refinance cost (including closing costs) should be no more than 2% of the loan amount. This ensures that refinancing doesn't significantly increase the overall debt without providing substantial benefits in savings or improved loan terms.

These rules of thumb give you quick guidelines to determine if refinancing is worth investigating further. However, the best decision always comes from combining these rules with a detailed break-even analysis that aligns with your specific goals and property strategy.

Risks and Drawbacks of Refinancing

Refinancing can offer substantial benefits, but it also comes with risks and drawbacks that should be carefully evaluated. Here are some of the primary risk factors to consider with both rate-and-term and cash-out refinancing.

- **Increased Costs and Fees** - Refinancing involves costs like loan origination fees, appraisal fees, and closing costs, which can add up quickly. While a rate-and-term refinance may have lower costs, a cash-out refinance typically incurs higher fees, adding to your loan balance and potentially impacting your return.
- **Tax Consequences** - Refinancing can affect your tax situation, especially if you're cashing out equity. Cash-out proceeds aren't typically taxed as income, but increasing debt may impact tax benefits like mortgage interest deductions. Always consult a tax advisor to understand any potential consequences that may apply to your unique situation.
- **Impact on Cash Flow** - A rate-and-term refinance can improve cash flow by lowering your monthly payment through a reduced interest rate or extended loan term. This often leads to improved cash flow and slightly lower reserve requirement due to the lower mortgage payment to keep the same number of months of reserves. In contrast, a cash-out refinance may increase your monthly payment if the new loan balance is significantly higher, which can strain cash flow and affect other risk factors.
- **Debt-to-Income (DTI) Ratio** - Both types of refinancing can impact your DTI ratio, which measures your monthly debt payments against your income. While a rate-and-term refinance may have minimal impact on DTI, a cash-out refinance that increases your loan balance will increase your DTI, potentially affecting your ability to qualify for future loans.

- **Debt Service Coverage Ratio (DSCR)** - DSCR measures the property's ability to cover its debt obligations with its income. A higher mortgage payment from a cash-out refinance could lower the DSCR, reducing your margin of safety and making it harder to secure additional financing if the property's income no longer covers the debt effectively.
- **Debt to Net Worth** - This ratio compares your total debt to your overall net worth. A cash-out refinance that increases your debt will raise this ratio, which could signal increased financial risk.
- **Debt to Liquid Net Worth** - This metric measures your debt relative to your liquid assets, such as cash or stocks. A cash-out refinance that increases debt without adding liquidity could weaken your liquidity position, leaving you more exposed to unexpected financial needs or market downturns.
- **Rent Resiliency™** - Rent Resiliency™ measures how much rent can drop before you have negative cash flow. A higher mortgage payment after a cash-out refinance could reduce Rent Resiliency™ by increasing the amount of rent needed before you'd have negative cash flow.
- **Price Resiliency™** - Price Resiliency™ reflects how much property prices can drop before you have negative equity. A higher loan balance from a cash-out refinance reduces Price Resiliency™, as it increases the sale price needed to break even or pay off the mortgage in a market downturn.
- **Months of Reserves** - Many investors prefer to keep a healthy reserve fund based on the number of months of expenses needed to cover a rental property's costs,

providing a safety net for unexpected repairs or vacancies. Lenders may also require a set number of months' worth of reserves as a condition for refinancing, particularly if your payment increases after a cash-out refinance. This could mean you'll need additional liquidity to maintain your desired or required reserve levels, potentially impacting your overall cash flow and flexibility.

Evaluating these risk factors helps ensure you make an informed decision about refinancing that aligns with your cash flow needs, risk tolerance, and long-term investment goals.

Refinancing Creatively Financed Deals

Refinancing a property acquired through creative financing presents specific considerations. Each method offers unique advantages for the initial purchase, but when transitioning to traditional financing, additional requirements and steps may be necessary.

Here's a look at common creative financing strategies and factors to consider when refinancing out of each:

- **Owner Financing** - In an owner-financed deal, the seller provides the loan directly, allowing you to make payments to them instead of a traditional lender. When refinancing, you'll need to pay off the seller's financing in full and qualify with a new lender, meeting typical requirements such as an appraisal and credit check.

However, if you've negotiated a substitution of collateral on the owner financing, you may be able to move the seller's loan to another property instead of paying it off.

- **Wrap Financing** - Wrap financing involves combining an existing mortgage with additional financing provided by the seller. In this arrangement, you often pay the seller a combined amount, and they use part of it to cover their mortgage. Refinancing a wrap loan requires paying off both the wrap and underlying loans.

- **Loan Assumption** - With a loan assumption, you formally take over the seller's mortgage with the lender's approval, and the loan is fully transferred into your name. To refinance, you'll need to meet standard loan requirements, but there's no issue with paying off the assumed loan since it's already in your name. Be mindful of any seasoning requirements, as some lenders may require you to hold the assumed loan for a certain period before refinancing.

- **Rent-to-Own Arrangements (Lease-Option and Lease-Purchase)** - In a rent-to-own arrangement, you lease the property with the option (or obligation) to buy at the end of the lease term. With a lease-option, you have the choice to purchase, whereas, in a lease-purchase, there's an implied obligation that you will buy the property. Since you don't own the property yet, refinancing doesn't apply. Instead, you'll exercise your option to buy using a purchase loan, similar to a traditional property purchase. This process requires you to meet down payment and closing cost requirements for a new loan.

- **Agreement-for-Deed, Bond-for-Deed, Contract-for-Deed, Installment Land Contracts** - In these arrangements, you make payments directly to the seller, and the legal title transfers to you upon fulfilling the contract. Contrary to some beliefs, these contracts can often be treated as refinances rather than purchases when seeking traditional financing. Because you hold equitable title during the contract period, you may be eligible for a rate-and-term refinance to pay off the existing contract without needing a traditional down payment, though you'll still need to meet lender requirements and cover closing costs.
- **Subject-To** - In a subject-to arrangement, you take ownership of the property subject to the seller's existing mortgage, which remains in place while you make the payments. When refinancing, you'll essentially be replacing the seller's old mortgage with your own, following standard refinance processes.

Each creative financing structure has specific benefits, but refinancing out of these arrangements often requires planning. The process may involve meeting lender requirements for seasoning, down payments, or title conditions, depending on the financing type. Understanding these nuances will help ensure a seamless transition from creative to conventional financing as your investment grows.

Using Spreadsheets to Analyze Returns Before and After Refinance

When contemplating a refinance, especially when it's not driven by an immediate need, it's wise to thoroughly assess the financial impact.

Utilizing a spreadsheet allows you to input various factors to compare your returns before and after refinancing. This detailed analysis helps you understand how refinancing could affect all the returns and return on investment calculations.

If you *need* to refinance because you require funds for an urgent matter like a health emergency, and it's your only available option, the decision is straightforward—you proceed with the refinance.

However, if you're in a position where refinancing is optional, taking the time to perform this mathematical analysis is both prudent and encouraged. It empowers you to make an informed decision that aligns with your financial goals.

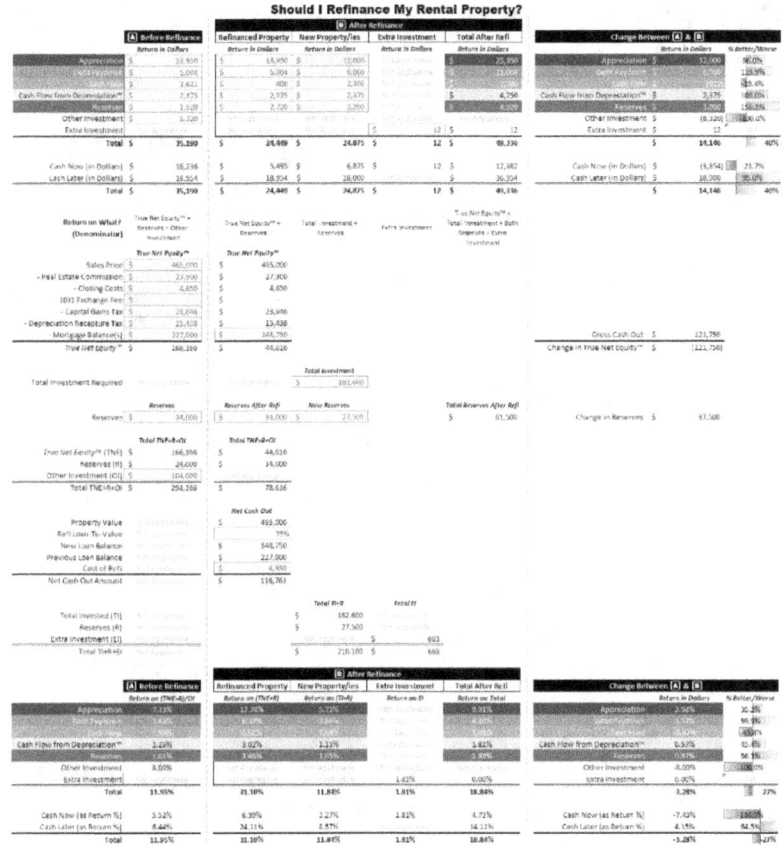

To assist you in this evaluation, you can download a customizable spreadsheet to follow along:

https://REFP.Info/jyasyw56

This tool will guide you through the process, allowing you to see the potential outcomes of refinancing versus maintaining your current loan, helping you make the best decision for your financial future.

Current Returns on Property You're Considering Refinancing

	A Before Refinance
	Return in Dollars
Appreciation	$ 13,950
Debt Paydown	$ 5,004
Cash Flow	$ 3,621
Cash Flow from Depreciation™	$ 2,375
Reserves	$ 1,920
Other Investment	$ 8,320
Extra Investment	Not Applicable
Total	$ 35,190

To evaluate the impact of refinancing on your rental property, you'll want to calculate the current returns you're earning. This gives you a "before" picture that can help you compare with the potential returns after refinancing.

Using the *Should I Refinance My Rental Property?* spreadsheet, start by entering estimates for each key component of your returns.

Here's how to gather and input these numbers:

- **Appreciation** - Appreciation refers to the increase in your property's market value over time. To estimate appreciation, think about how much you expect the property to increase in value over the next year. If you're unsure, using a 3% annual appreciation rate is a conservative estimate, as this aligns with the historical long-term average nationwide. Enter this percentage or dollar amount in the spreadsheet to capture your expected return from appreciation.

- **Debt Paydown** - Debt paydown represents the reduction in your mortgage principal balance as you make monthly payments. Check your latest mortgage statement for the amount of principal paid down in the most recent month. Then, multiply this figure by 12 to estimate the annual debt paydown. Keep in mind that this is a conservative estimate, as your principal reduction typically grows slightly each month on a fully amortizing loan.

- **Cash Flow** - Cash flow is the net income generated by your rental property after covering all expenses, including mortgage payments, taxes, insurance, vacancy, property management and maintenance costs. Estimate the total cash flow you expect over the next year by looking at your rental income minus these expenses. Enter the annual cash flow amount in the spreadsheet to see how much return you're earning from cash flow alone.

- **Cash Flow from Depreciation™** - *Cash Flow from Depreciation™* is a tax benefit that comes from the IRS's allowance to deduct a portion of your property's value over time. This deduction reduces your taxable income, effectively increasing your net cash flow. Calculate this by estimating the tax savings you receive from depreciation on the property, and enter the estimated annual benefit in the spreadsheet. This provides a realistic view of your net cash flow return, factoring in tax savings.

- **Reserves** - Reserves are funds set aside to cover unforeseen property expenses, such as repairs or vacancies. Look at the amount you've set aside in reserves for the property and enter the estimated annual return you're earning on this money. For example, if your reserves are in a savings account, assume around 1% per year, or if they're invested in an index fund, you might estimate around 8% per year.

Once you've entered these numbers in the spreadsheet, you'll have a clear understanding of your current returns on the property you're considering refinancing. This "before" analysis is essential for determining whether a refinance will improve your overall investment performance.

Returns on Other Investment

In the *Should I Refinance My Rental Property?* spreadsheet, the section for the returns you're earning on "Other Investment" allows you to factor in any additional capital you might use alongside your refinance proceeds. This is especially relevant if the refinance alone doesn't provide enough funds to cover a new investment or property acquisition.

Here's how to handle this section:

- **Determine if Additional Capital is Needed** - If the proceeds from the refinance cover your investment needs, you can leave this section blank. However, if you require additional capital from other sources to complete a new purchase, you'll want to enter those details here.

- **Estimate Expected Returns on Additional Investment Capital** - For an accurate picture of your overall returns, enter the estimated annual return on this additional capital. This includes any funds from other investments that you're allocating toward the property or properties. If, for example, you're pulling funds from a stock portfolio, you might estimate an 8% annual return. Enter the expected return in dollars to reflect what you would have earned had you left the funds in their original investment.
- **Calculate Annual Returns in Dollars** - Finally, determine the total expected returns from these additional funds over the next year and enter this dollar amount in the spreadsheet. Including this figure ensures that the "before" picture accurately represents the opportunity cost of using other investment capital alongside the refinance proceeds.

Adding returns on other investment capital will help you see the full scope of your starting financial position, enabling a more complete comparison of potential returns after refinancing.

Expected Returns on Property After Refinancing

	B	After Refinance		
Refinanced Property	**New Property/ies**	**Extra Investment**	**Total After Refi**
Return in Dollars	*Return in Dollars*	*Return in Dollars*	*Return in Dollars*
$ 13,950	$ 12,000	Not Applicable	$ 25,950
$ 5,004	$ 6,000	Not Applicable	$ 11,004
$ 400	$ 2,300	Not Applicable	$ 2,700
$ 2,375	$ 2,375	Not Applicable	$ 4,750
$ 2,720	$ 2,200	Not Applicable	$ 4,920
Not Applicable	Not Applicable	Not Applicable	Not Applicable
Not Applicable	Not Applicable	$ 12	$ 12
$ 24,449	$ 24,875	$ 12	$ 49,336

In the *Should I Refinance My Rental Property?* spreadsheet, the expected returns on the original property (or properties) after refinancing section helps you project your new returns based on the updated financial structure post-refinance.

This gives you a comparative "after" snapshot for assessing whether refinancing improves your property's performance.

Here's how to approach each field:

- **Appreciation** - Appreciation represents the anticipated increase in the property's value over the next year. Since refinancing typically doesn't impact the property's market value, your expected appreciation rate will likely remain the same as in your initial analysis.
- **Debt Paydown** - Debt paydown reflects the principal you'll reduce over the next year on your refinanced loan. This may change depending on the new loan's balance, interest rate, and term. Even if the loan balance doesn't

increase significantly, an adjustment to the interest rate or term will alter your monthly principal reduction. Review your new loan's amortization schedule to find the expected annual principal paydown, and enter this amount in the spreadsheet.

- **Cash Flow** - Cash flow often changes after a refinance, especially if you're doing a cash-out refinance that increases your loan balance. While a rate-and-term refinance may improve cash flow by reducing monthly payments, cash-out refinances can reduce cash flow if they lead to higher monthly payments. If your refinance results in a lower interest rate or an extended term, this could offset the impact on cash flow. Estimate the annual cash flow after refinancing and enter it here to see how your monthly returns are expected to change.

- **Cash Flow from Depreciation™** - *Cash Flow from Depreciation™* is the tax benefit from property depreciation. Since depreciation is based on the original purchase price and the IRS's depreciation schedule, this typically remains unchanged by refinancing. Enter the same annual depreciation benefit you recorded before refinancing, as it will still apply to your post-refinance cash flow.

- **Reserves** - Your reserve requirements may increase if your monthly expenses rise after refinancing. For instance, if your new mortgage payment is higher, and you maintain reserves equivalent to a set number of months of expenses, you'll need to allocate more to reserves. Estimate the return you're earning on this larger reserve amount—whether it's in a savings account earning around 1% or in investments like index funds at around 8%. Enter this expected return to capture any adjustment in reserve growth due to refinancing.

These expected returns after refinancing will provide a complete view of how the refinance impacts each area of property performance.

Expected Returns on New Property or Properties

If you plan to purchase additional properties using the proceeds from a cash-out refinance (and any other investment funds), you'll want to enter the expected returns for each property into the *Should I Refinance My Rental Property?* spreadsheet.

This helps give you a complete "after" picture of your total portfolio performance post-refinance.

Here's how to consider each field:

- **Appreciation** - Appreciation refers to the increase in market value for your newly purchased property or properties. Estimate the annual appreciation rate for the new property based on market conditions or use a general long-term average, like 3%. This figure will give you a baseline for potential property value growth over the next year. Enter this annual appreciation amount in the spreadsheet.
- **Debt Paydown** - Debt paydown measures the reduction in your mortgage principal over the year, which builds equity in your property. Check the amortization schedule

for your new loan(s) to see how much principal you're expected to pay down in the first year, based on the interest rate and loan term. Enter the estimated annual debt paydown amount in the spreadsheet.

- **Cash Flow** - Cash flow is the net income generated by your property after covering all expenses, including mortgage payments, taxes, insurance, and maintenance. Estimate the annual cash flow you expect to earn from the new property, keeping in mind any rental income projections and expense considerations. Enter the projected annual cash flow to calculate its contribution to your overall returns.

- **Cash Flow from Depreciation™** - *Cash Flow from Depreciation™* is the tax benefit derived from property depreciation. Based on IRS rules, you can deduct a portion of the property's purchase price (not including the value of the land) over 27.5 years for residential rental properties. Calculate the annual depreciation amount for tax purposes and estimate the resulting cash flow benefit from tax savings. Enter this amount to see how it impacts your post-refinance returns.

- **Reserves** - Reserves are the funds set aside to cover unexpected expenses for the new property, such as repairs or vacancy periods. If you keep reserves equivalent to a specific number of months' expenses, calculate the reserve amount needed for the new property. Next, estimate the annual return on these reserves based on where the funds are held (e.g., 1% in a savings account or around 8% if invested in an index fund). Enter this expected return in the spreadsheet to complete the analysis.

32

By entering these expected returns on your new property or properties, you'll gain a clearer view of the financial impact of the refinance.

Returns on Extra Investment

In the *Should I Refinance My Rental Property?* spreadsheet, the "Extra Investment" section allows you to account for any surplus capital left over after completing a cash-out refinance and making planned property purchases. This "extra investment" represents funds not needed for new acquisitions or reserves, which can now be invested elsewhere.

Here's how to approach this section:

- **Extra Investment Defined** - Once you've used your cash-out refinance proceeds to purchase additional properties and allocate reserves, any remaining capital becomes "extra investment." This is your surplus cash, not directly linked to property purchases or refinancing costs, which you can put to work in other investments.
- **Estimating Returns on Extra Investment** - For the spreadsheet, estimate the expected annual return on this extra investment. If the funds remain in a savings account, assume around 1% annual growth; if invested in stocks or bonds, you might project a return closer to 6–8% based on historical averages. Enter this estimated return to see how your surplus capital contributes to your total post-refinance returns.

What's the Difference Between Other Investment and Extra Investment?

"Other Investment" refers to additional capital from outside the cash-out refinance that you might use to buy new property or cover other costs. After meeting these needs, any leftover "Other Investment" becomes "Extra Investment," where you'll analyze its potential returns.

If you included "Other Investment" in your property purchase, consider reducing the extra investment field to reflect only the minimal amount needed. This avoids surplus capital that isn't earning returns or being allocated efficiently.

Factoring in returns on extra investment gives you a fuller picture of your capital allocation, helping you assess if any surplus funds are effectively enhancing your overall investment returns.

Before and After in Dollars

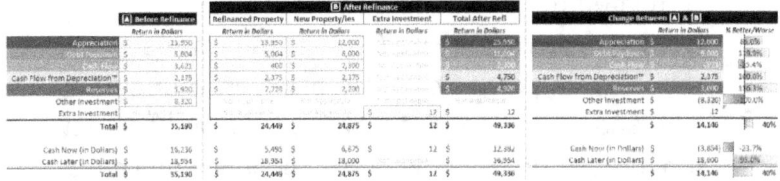

The *Should I Refinance My Rental Property?* spreadsheet provides a clear summary of your returns both before and after the refinance. This summary highlights how each component of your returns has changed as a result of the refinance, helping you see the financial impact in dollar terms.

The top of the spreadsheet compares the following categories of returns in dollars from "before" (the current setup) to "after" (the post-refinance scenario):

- **Property Returns and Additional Investments** - The spreadsheet shows the total returns in dollars from the property you're refinancing, any additional properties acquired with the refinance proceeds, and any surplus capital in extra investments. This overview allows you to see your combined return in dollar amounts across all invested funds.

- **Return Differences in Key Areas** - The spreadsheet breaks down the differences in returns across essential categories, allowing you to see how each area changes after refinancing:

  - **Appreciation** - How much more appreciation (property value increase) you might see by using a cash-out refinance to purchase additional properties compared to not refinancing.

  - **Debt Paydown** - The difference in principal reduction over the next year between your current loan and the refinanced loan(s), including any new properties purchased with the refinance proceeds.

  - **Cash Flow** - The change in net cash flow on the refinanced property, considering any shifts in loan payments, and the additional cash flow generated from any new properties.

- Cash Flow from Depreciation™ - The increase in tax benefits from depreciation, factoring in both the original property and any additional properties acquired with refinance proceeds.
- Reserves - The difference in the returns earned on reserves, accounting for any changes in the reserve amounts required for both the refinanced property and newly acquired properties.
- Other Investment/Extra Investment - The change in returns from any remaining capital (extra investment) that is invested outside of property purchases or from any other investment capital needed to fund new acquisitions.

The spreadsheet also provides a total of all these returns, summing the "before" and "after" scenarios to give a complete view of your returns in dollar terms.

- **Percentage Change Overview** - Finally, the spreadsheet calculates the percentage difference in each of these categories, giving you a snapshot of whether the returns in each area are better or worse than they were pre-refinance. It also includes the total overall percentage change, so you can quickly assess the refinance's impact on your total returns.

By comparing these before-and-after figures in dollars and percentages, you can make a more informed decision about whether refinancing aligns with your investment goals and enhances the performance of your rental portfolio.

Different Types of Returns: Not All Are Created Equal

When evaluating returns, it's important to recognize that not all returns offer the same value or flexibility. Each type of return—Appreciation, Debt Paydown, Cash Flow, *Cash Flow from Depreciation™*, Reserves, and Other Investment/Extra Investment—has unique characteristics that influence how and when you can use them.

Cash Now Returns vs. Cash Later Returns

Cash Now (in Dollars)	$	10,299	$	5,495	$	6,875	$	12	$	12,382	Cash Now (in Dollars)	$	(1,854)	-21.7%
Cash Later (in Dollars)	$	18,594	$	18,554	$	18,000			$	36,554	Cash Later (in Dollars)	$	18,000	55.0%
Total	$	15,190	$	24,449	$	24,875	$	12	$	49,136		$	14,146	-8/%

Some returns are readily accessible, or "Cash Now" returns, meaning you can spend or reinvest them in the short term. Examples include:

- **Cash Flow** - The immediate net income you receive from rental operations.
- **Cash Flow from Depreciation™** - The tax benefit that reduces taxable income, effectively boosting your spendable cash.
- **Return on Reserves** - The return you earn from funds set aside for unexpected expenses.
- **Return on Other Investment/Extra Investment** - Earnings from capital invested outside of your property, like savings, stocks, or bonds.

These returns are available to you immediately, helping cover expenses or reinvesting in other areas. In contrast, "Cash Later" returns are long-term and usually only accessible upon sale or refinance of the property. These include:

- **Appreciation** - The growth in property value over time.
- **Debt Paydown** - The reduction in loan principal, which builds equity but doesn't provide immediate cash flow.

Cash Later returns are essential for wealth building but are less flexible since they can't be spent or reinvested until a future event.

Impact of Refinancing on Cash Now vs. Cash Later

When refinancing, consider how the shift in returns affects your immediate cash flow versus long-term equity.

For instance, increasing leverage through refinancing and acquiring additional properties can often increase Cash Later returns from Appreciation and Debt Paydown but may reduce Cash Now returns, such as Cash Flow. If your initial property provided a healthy Cash Now return, and refinancing shifts most of the return to Cash Later, it may impact your short-term liquidlty or spending goals.

Speculative vs. Certain Returns

Not all returns are equally reliable. Certain returns depend heavily on external factors, making them speculative. For example:

- **Appreciation** - Dependent on the real estate market and economic conditions.
- **Cash Flow** - Relies on stable rental income, low vacancy, and manageable expenses. Factors like tenant turnover or unexpected repairs can impact this.

Other returns are more predictable and less market-dependent:

- **Debt Paydown** - This occurs as long as you make mortgage payments, regardless of market fluctuations.
- **Tax Benefits from Depreciation** - The tax deduction for depreciation is predictable, barring tax law changes, and provides consistent savings.

Some returns could go either way depending on what they're invested in like the return on reserves, other investments and extra investments. If they're in savings, they're probably more predictable and less market dependent. If they invested in stocks, they're probably less predictable and more market dependent.

The *Should I Refinance My Rental Property?* spreadsheet breaks down returns into Cash Now and Cash Later, allowing you to see how these balances change post-refinance. This can be critical for determining if a refinance aligns with your financial needs and investment goals, balancing immediate cash accessibility with long-term equity growth.

Return in Dollars Versus Return on Investment

When evaluating your property's performance, it's important to distinguish between the return in dollars and the return on what you have invested. These two measures provide different insights into how effectively your property is working for you.

- **Return in Dollars** - So far, we've discussed the total dollar returns from your property or properties: appreciation, cash flow, debt paydown, tax benefits plus the returns from other/extra investments. While knowing the dollar amount of return is essential, it doesn't provide a complete picture.
- **Why Return on Investment Matters** - To truly understand how well your investment is performing, you need to look at the some measure of the return on how much you have invested. This return on how much you have invested measures efficiency by showing what percentage of your investment's current value is being earned back each year.
- **Calculating Return for New Purchases** - For properties you've just acquired, calculating return on investment is straightforward. You take the total dollar returns and divide by the total amount you invested to acquire the property, often called **Total**

Investment/Total Invested on *The World's Greatest Real Estate Deal Analysis Spreadsheet™*. For newly acquired properties like those purchased with cash-out refinance proceeds, this method provides a meaningful way to gauge returns on the amount you needed to invest to acquire the property.

- **Long-Term Property Ownership and ROI** - However, as time passes, the initial investment amount becomes less relevant. Here's an example: Suppose you bought a property 30 years ago for $50,000, with a $10,000 down payment. Now, the property is worth $120,000, and the mortgage is fully paid off. Calculating ROI based on the original $10,000 down payment no longer accurately reflects the current efficiency of the investment. That initial investment might show how well the property performed historically, but it doesn't help us measure its performance today on how much you currently have tied up in the property.

- **Assessing Current Performance with ROI** - To measure today's performance, you'd look at the dollar returns for the coming year and divide by the total amount of money you currently have invested in the property. This updated figure provides a realistic sense of how effectively your property is working for you now, not just when you bought it.

- **Equity as a Starting Point, But Not the Full Picture** - Some investors measure the return on their current investment by dividing returns by the property's current equity, which moves in the right direction but isn't a complete solution. Equity is alone doesn't consider the actual cost to access that equity (such as taxes, selling expenses, and other transaction costs), making it only an approximate measure.

Using return on the amount you have invested in the property alongside dollar returns lets you evaluate how effectively both new and seasoned properties are performing, allowing you to make better-informed decisions about whether to hold, refinance, or reposition your investments for maximum efficiency.

Equity

Equity represents the difference between your property's market value and the amount you owe on it. In other words, it's the portion of the property you "own" outright.

However, equity is also somewhat imaginary. The number we call "equity" on paper is rarely fully accessible. To access it, whether through refinancing or selling, you'll encounter various costs that reduce the actual amount you receive.

- **Refinancing Limitations** - If you refinance, lenders typically cap your loan amount based on a percentage of the property's value, known as the loan-to-value (LTV) ratio. Even if you refinance up to 100% LTV, refinance costs will further reduce the amount you receive.
- **Selling Limitations** - If you choose to sell the property, accessing equity will require paying a range of costs. These often include real estate commissions, closing costs, potential 1031 tax-deferred exchange fees, and

taxes on capital gains and depreciation recapture. Each of these expenses reduces the cash you can actually access from your property's equity.

Since "equity" is a rough estimate, you may want a more practical measure that reflects actual, accessible value. This leads us to a concept beyond just equity on paper: how much of your equity you can realistically access after all costs are considered. This approach helps you see the effective value of your property investment when factoring in transaction costs and tax obligations.

True Net Equity™

	True Net Equity™	True Net Equity™
Sales Price	$ 465,000	$ 465,000
- Real Estate Commission	$ 27,900	$ 27,900
- Closing Costs	$ 4,650	$ 4,650
- 1031 Exchange Fee	$ -	$ -
- Capital Gains Tax	$ 23,646	$ 23,646
- Depreciation Recapture Tax	$ 15,438	$ 15,438
- Mortgage Balance(s)	$ 227,000	$ 348,750
True Net Equity™	$ 166,366	$ 44,616

True Net Equity™ gives you a more realistic view of how much equity you actually have in a property by accounting for all the costs that reduce the amount you can access. Instead of just looking at the difference between your property's value and mortgage balance, *True Net Equity™* considers your share of closing costs, real estate commissions, and any taxes you would owe on gains and depreciation recapture. If you plan to defer taxes, it also includes 1031 exchange fees. This calculation shows you how much you'd genuinely "walk away with" if you sold the property today.

In other words, *True Net Equity™* represents the cash you'd have on hand after all selling or refinancing expenses. It provides a clearer picture of what you truly have invested in the deal and helps you gauge how the investment is currently performing.

To calculate *True Net Equity™* on the *Should I Refinance My Rental Property?* spreadsheet, you'll need:

- **Sales Price** - The estimated market value of the property.
- **Real Estate Commission** - The fee paid to agents upon selling.
- **Closing Costs** - Expenses related to the sale, such as title and escrow fees.
- **1031 Exchange Fee** - If you defer taxes through a 1031 exchange, include the intermediary's fee.
- **Capital Gains Tax** - Taxes owed on the increase in value since purchase.
- **Depreciation Recapture Tax** - Taxes on the depreciated value claimed over the years.
- **Mortgage Balance** - The remaining amount owed on the property loan.

Subtracting these costs from the sales price gives you *True Net Equity™*—the actual amount you'd net from a sale or the "real" investment value in the property. Calculating this both before and after a refinance gives you an accurate basis for assessing your returns, making *True Net Equity™* the foundation for a more precise *Return on True Net Equity™* calculation, which we'll explore shortly.

Total Investment Required

			Total Invested	
Total Investment Required	Not Applicable	Not Applicable	$	182,600

Total Investment represents the full amount you've invested to acquire a property, including all initial and necessary expenses.

While we often calculate returns using *True Net Equity™* for properties owned for some time, many investors use the initial *Total Investment* when calculating returns on newly purchased properties. This method tends to be more conservative, as initial costs are often significantly higher than what *True Net Equity™* would show after accounting for sale expenses.

When you're buying new properties with cash-out refinance proceeds, we'll use the *Total Investment* method to calculate returns. While this approach may slightly understate performance due to a larger denominator, it provides a reliable snapshot of the initial investment's performance.

On the *Should I Refinance My Rental Property?* spreadsheet, you'll enter the *Total Investment* required to acquire any new property purchased with refinance proceeds. You can gather the *Total Investment* figure from

The World's Greatest Real Estate Deal Analysis Spreadsheet™, which includes:

- **Down Payment** - The initial cash contribution toward the property's purchase price.
- **Closing Costs** - All fees associated with finalizing the transaction, such as title fees, appraisal fees, and lender fees.
- **Seller Concessions** - Any credits provided by the seller to offset allowable closing costs.
- **Rent Ready Costs** - Expenses needed to make the property rental-ready, including repairs or necessary upgrades.
- **Cumulative Negative Cash Flow** - If the property has negative cash flow due to a smaller down payment, this is the projected total of negative cash flow before rent increases push cash flow to eventually be positive.

By accurately capturing each of these costs, *Total Investment* provides a comprehensive measure of your initial capital outlay, allowing you to track performance on newly acquired properties alongside existing assets.

Reserves

	Reserves	Reserves After Refi	New Reserves	Total Reserves After Refi
Reserves	$ 24,000	$ 34,000	$ 27,500	$ 61,500

Reserves are the funds you set aside to cover unexpected expenses for your rental property, such as repairs, vacancies, or emergencies. While we've already accounted for the return on these reserves in the *Should I Refinance*

My Rental Property? spreadsheet, we now need to record the actual dollar amount in reserves. Including these funds in your calculations provides a more accurate view of your total investment, as reserves are an essential part of a prudent real estate investment strategy.

On the spreadsheet, enter the dollar amount you currently have set aside in reserves. You'll need to input reserve amounts for:

- **Pre-Refinance Reserves** - The amount in reserves for the property or properties you're considering refinancing. This initial figure reflects the capital you've set aside to maintain the property before refinancing.
- **Post-Refinance Reserves** - The reserve amount required after refinancing. This amount often increases if you're maintaining a fixed number of months' worth of expenses in reserves and your monthly payments have risen due to the refinance.
- **New Property Reserves** - The reserve amount for any new property or properties acquired with cash-out refinance proceeds. Ensure you allocate reserves for these properties to cover future unexpected costs, following your reserve guidelines.

By incorporating reserve amounts for both existing and newly acquired properties, the spreadsheet provides a clearer picture of your true investment, giving you a more complete basis for evaluating returns on investment across all investments directly involved in your refinance.

Other Investment

	Total TNE+R+OI		Total TNE+R+OI
True Net Equity™ (TNE)	$ 166,366	$	44,616
Reserves (R)	$ 24,000	$	34,000
Other Investment (OI)	$ 104,000	Not Applicable	
Total TNE+R+OI	$ 294,366	$	78,616

In addition to your property and reserves, the *Should I Refinance My Rental Property?* spreadsheet includes a section for *Other Investment*—any additional capital you have invested outside of your rental property. This could include investments in stocks, bonds, or other assets unrelated to the property itself.

While we've already discussed the return you're currently earning on these *Other Investments*, the spreadsheet now requires you to enter the total dollar amount you have in *Other Investment*. This figure is essential for calculating accurate return on investment metrics, as it accounts for all capital working within your investment strategy.

By including this additional investment amount, the spreadsheet offers a more comprehensive view of your portfolio's performance, allowing for a balanced analysis of returns from both property-specific assets and external investments.

Refi Loan-To-Value

		Net Cash Out
Property Value	Not Applicable	$ 465,000
Refi Loan-To-Value	Not Applicable	75%
New Loan Balance	Not Applicable	$ 348,750
Previous Loan Balance	Not Applicable	$ 227,000
Cost of Refi	Not Applicable	$ 4,988
Net Cash Out Amount	Not Applicable	$ 116,763

In the *Should I Refinance My Rental Property?* spreadsheet, you'll be prompted to enter the **Refinance Loan-to-Value (LTV)** ratio. This percentage represents the loan amount relative to the property's appraised value at the time of refinancing. For example, an 75% LTV means the loan amount is 75% of the property's appraised value.

Cost of Refi

In the *Should I Refinance My Rental Property?* spreadsheet, you'll need to enter the **Cost of Refinance**—the total expenses associated with completing the refinance. This figure is essential, as it will be subtracted from the cash available for reinvestment post-refinance, affecting your overall return on investment.

Refinance costs typically include a percentage of the loan amount, known as **origination fees**, as well as **fixed costs** that don't vary based on loan size, like appraisal fees, title company closing costs, and administrative fees. For instance, you might incur a 1% origination fee on a

$200,000 loan, plus fixed costs of around $2,000 for title, appraisal, and processing.

By inputting these costs into the spreadsheet, you get an accurate view of your net investment after refinancing, giving you a clearer picture of the funds available to deploy and how much the refinance affects your property's financial performance.

Before and After Return on Amount Invested

[A] Before Refinance	[B] After Refinance				Change Between [A] & [B]	
	Refinanced Property	New Property/ies	Extra Investment	Total After Refi		
Return on (TNE+R)/OI	Return on (TNE+R)	Return on (TI+R)	Return on OI	Return on Total	Return in Dollars	% Better/Worse
Appreciation 2.93%	17.36%	3.71%		9.91%	Appreciation 2.58%	10.3%
Cash Flow from Depreciation 1.25%	3.62%	1.15%		1.81%	Cash Flow from Depreciation 0.37%	40.4%
Other Investment 6.00%	1.44%	1.05%	0.00%	1.00%	Other Investment -8.00%	-100.0%
Extra Investment			1.81%		Extra Investment 0.00%	
Total 11.95%	31.10%	11.84%	1.81%	19.84%	Total -1.28%	-2%
Cash Now (as Return %) 5.50%	6.99%	3.27%	1.81%	4.73%	Cash Now (as Return %) -7.43%	
Cash Later (as Return %) 6.44%	24.11%	8.57%		14.11%	Cash Later (as Return %) 4.15%	64.5%
Total 11.95%	31.10%	11.84%	1.81%	19.84%	Total -1.28%	-27%

The *Should I Refinance My Rental Property?* spreadsheet compares your *Return on Amount Invested* before and after refinancing. This calculation is valuable, but it combines slightly different bases: it uses the initial cash investment for newly acquired properties, True Net Equity™ for established properties, and includes reserves in both cases. Additionally, it accounts for either Other Investment or Extra Investment funds, depending on the scenario you're evaluating.

Because of these varied approaches, the *Return on Amount Invested* calculation can be seen as an "apples-to-oranges" comparison, whereas the *Return in Dollars* is a truer "apples-to-apples" look at how much each dollar invested earns in absolute terms.

As George Box famously noted, "All models are wrong, but some are useful." While this analysis might not provide a perfect one-to-one comparison, it remains a practical tool to evaluate how efficiently each part of your investment performs across different stages, helping you make more informed decisions.

Not Buying Additional Properties

If you're refinancing but not planning to purchase additional properties with the proceeds, the *Should I Refinance My Rental Property?* spreadsheet allows you to adjust the analysis to reflect this strategy.

- **Zero Out Returns for New Properties** - In the spreadsheet, you can set the *Return in Dollars* fields for any new property or properties to zero. This includes fields for Appreciation, Debt Paydown, Cash Flow, *Cash Flow from Depreciation™*, Reserves, and the *Total Investment* and *New Reserves* sections. By zeroing these out, you indicate that no funds will be allocated to additional property purchases.
- **Allocate Cash-Out Proceeds to Extra Investment** - Enter the cash-out refinance proceeds into the *Extra Investment* field. From there, you can estimate the expected return on this capital based on where you'll invest it, such as savings accounts, stocks, or bonds.

- **Paying Off Debt** - If you're using refinance proceeds to pay off debt, you can estimate the "return" on these funds by using the interest rate of the debt you're eliminating as the *Extra Investment* return. This method gives you a measure of how much you're effectively earning by reducing your debt expenses.

This approach helps you accurately assess the financial impact of a refinance even without purchasing additional properties, allowing you to project returns based on alternative investments or debt reduction strategies.

Buying Down Your Mortgage Interest Rate When Refinancing

When refinancing, you may have the option to buy down your mortgage interest rate by paying points upfront. Each point typically costs 1% of the loan amount and can reduce your interest rate by around 0.125% to 0.25%, depending on the lender.

Here are some key considerations for deciding whether a rate buy-down is a good move for you:

- **Long-Term Savings vs. Upfront Cost** - Buying down the interest rate means paying more upfront to secure a lower monthly payment over the life of the loan. This can make sense if you plan to hold the property long enough to recoup these upfront costs through interest savings. However, if you plan to sell or refinance again within a few years, you may not break even on the buy-down cost.

- **Extra Cost of a Rate Buy-Down** - The upfront cost for buying down your rate adds to the total cost of the refinance. For example, on a $200,000 loan, one point would cost $2,000. Consider how much you're paying per point and how much the rate reduction impacts your monthly payment to determine if it's worth the expense.
- **Rolling Buy-Down Costs into the Loan** - In many cases, lenders allow you to roll the cost of buying down the rate into the loan amount, spreading out the expense over time. This option can improve your cash flow at closing but will slightly increase the loan balance, so it's essential to weigh the total long-term impact.

Buying down the rate can be a powerful tool to lower interest costs and ultimately improve cash flow, but it's most effective when it aligns with your long-term property strategy and holding period. Calculating the break-even period for the buy-down helps ensure it's a cost-effective decision.

Refinancing When Rates Are Higher

Refinancing typically appeals most when interest rates are lower than your current rate, allowing you to reduce your monthly payment. However, if interest rates have risen since you first financed your rental property, refinancing can present a dilemma—especially if your property has accumulated substantial equity.

Fixed-Rate Protection

Fixed-rate financing provides stability by locking in your interest rate, protecting you from future rate hikes. If rates drop, you have the option to refinance and lower your payment. This "ratchet effect" means you can secure a better rate, but you never have to settle for a worse one.

Evaluating High-Rate Refinancing

If current interest rates are higher than your existing rate but your property's return on equity (ROE) is dropping due to increased equity, you face a tough choice. For refinancing to make sense, the purpose for accessing your equity must offer returns that outweigh the impact of a higher interest rate. If you can achieve significantly higher returns by reinvesting cash-out proceeds—perhaps in new property acquisitions or other high-yield investments—it may be worth considering despite the rate increase.

Accessing Equity Without Refinancing

If the higher rate makes refinancing unattractive, consider tapping into your equity through a home equity line of credit (HELOC) or a second mortgage. Both options allow you to access cash while preserving your low fixed rate on the primary loan.

- **HELOC (Home Equity Line of Credit)** - A HELOC acts as a revolving line of credit, allowing you to borrow only what you need, pay it down, and borrow again as needed. HELOCs often have variable interest rates, meaning they can fluctuate with the market. However, you'll only pay interest on the amount you borrow, and you keep your existing mortgage at its current rate.
- **Second Mortgage** - A second mortgage provides a lump-sum loan that sits "behind" your original mortgage. Unlike a HELOC, the interest rate on a second mortgage is typically fixed, offering predictable payments. This can be beneficial if you need a set amount of cash upfront and want a consistent monthly payment.

Both options help you access equity without losing the benefit of your low-rate primary mortgage, enabling you to optimize returns without sacrificing your current cash flow.

Refinancing and Asset Protection

Refinancing can play a strategic role in asset protection for real estate investors by reducing the attractiveness of your property as a target for lawsuits and creditors. By increasing the loan balance on your property through a cash-out refinance, you reduce the visible equity that could otherwise be seen as an asset worth pursuing in legal action. This added leverage may discourage potential claimants, as there appears to be less equity to target.

Additionally, refinancing provides you with liquid funds that can be redirected to other investments, ideally in structures that offer enhanced protection, such as limited liability companies (LLCs) or trusts. Diversifying your equity across multiple investments or asset classes, rather than keeping it concentrated in one property, can provide another layer of protection by spreading risk.

Refinancing, when combined with sound asset protection structures, helps you shield your wealth, providing both liquidity and a strategic barrier against potential liabilities.

BONUS CHAPTERS

Introduction to Real Estate Deal Analysis

Analyzing real estate deals can be a daunting task, but with the right tools and knowledge, it becomes much more manageable. One powerful tool we recommend is *The World's Greatest Real Estate Deal Analysis Spreadsheet*™. This spreadsheet is designed to help you evaluate the financial viability of real estate investments with ease and precision.

In our book, *How to Analyze Real Estate Deals*, we delve deep into the intricacies of deal analysis, providing step-by-step instructions and expert insights. This introduction aims to give you a high-level overview of the process and how to effectively use the spreadsheet to make informed investment decisions.

The spreadsheet allows you to input various data points such as purchase price, mortgage details, monthly income, and annual expenses. It then performs complex calculations to provide you with key metrics like cash flow, return on investment (ROI), and internal rate of return (IRR).

By leveraging this tool, you can:

- Quickly assess the profitability of potential deals.
- Compare multiple investment opportunities.
- Make data-driven decisions to maximize your returns.

Whether you're a seasoned investor or just starting out, understanding how to analyze real estate deals is crucial for success.

Download Spreadsheet for Free

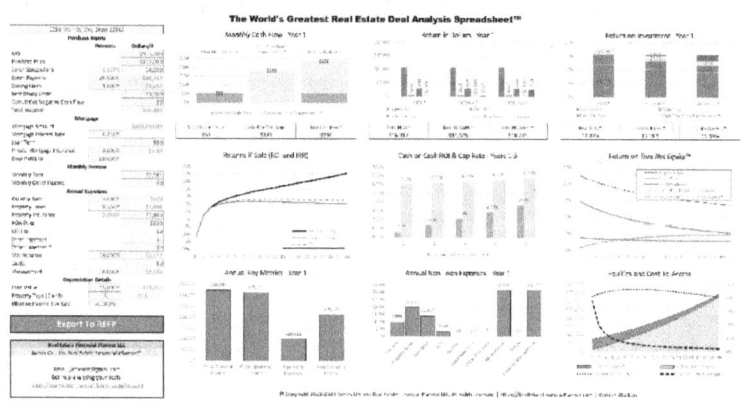

Unlock the full potential of your real estate investments by downloading *The World's Greatest Real Estate Deal Analysis Spreadsheet*™ for free.

Get your copy at: https://REFP.info/spreadsheet

We recommend always keeping an unedited, fresh copy on your hard drive in case you can't download the spreadsheet in the future.

Before analyzing a property, always make a new copy.

Spreadsheet Inputs

Entering the inputs into the spreadsheet is simple. Here's what you need to know:

- The manila fields indicate where you should input your data.
- The gray background with blue text shows the calculations that are automatically performed for you.

First, please name the deal that you're analyzing in the field just above the "Purchase Inputs". This will allow you to know which deal you're looking at if you're considering analyzing multiple deals or one deal multiple ways.

Purchase Inputs

Before we dive into the specifics of analyzing a real estate deal, let's go over the inputs required for the spreadsheet. These inputs will be divided into two columns: one for percentages and one for dollar amounts (or numbers).

Understanding what to enter in each field is crucial for accurately analyzing your deal. Let's go over what to put in each field next.

- **ARV** - Enter the After Repair Value, which is the estimated value of the property after all repairs and improvements have been made.
- **Purchase Price** - Enter the amount you are paying to acquire the property from the seller.
- **Seller Concessions** - Enter any financial concessions or incentives that the seller has agreed to provide, such as covering closing costs or offering repair credits.
- **Down Payment** - Enter the initial amount you will pay out-of-pocket towards the purchase of the property. Be sure to check out our guide on creative ways to come up with down payments for rental properties.
- **Closing Costs** - Enter the total costs associated with closing the real estate transaction, including title insurance, attorney fees, and other related expenses.
- **Rent Ready Costs** - Enter the expenses required to make the property ready for tenants, such as cleaning, repairs, and any necessary upgrades.
- **Cumulative Negative Cash Flow** - If you have negative cash flow enter the total cumulative amount of negative cash flow you anticipate before the property becomes cash flow positive. We recommend you set this aside to reduce risk. You may also want to check out our book on *How to Improve Cash Flow on Rental Properties* to get rid of negative cash flow on your properties.
- **Total Invested** - This is calculated for you. It is the cumulative amount of money you have invested in the

property, including **Down Payment, Closing Costs, Rent Ready Costs, Cumulative Negative Cash Flow**, minus any **Seller Concessions** you received from the seller.

Mortgage Inputs

To accurately analyze your real estate deal, it's essential to input detailed information about your mortgage and financing. These inputs will help calculate your monthly payments, interest costs, and overall financial commitment. Here's what you'll need to enter:

- **Mortgage Amount** - This is calculated for you. It is the total amount of money you are borrowing to finance the purchase of the property.
- **Mortgage Interest Rate** - Enter the annual interest rate for your mortgage. This is the percentage of the loan amount that you will pay as interest each year.
- **Loan Term** - Enter the duration of your mortgage loan in months. 360 months is a 30-year loan. This is the period over which you will repay the loan.
- **Private Mortgage Insurance** - Enter the monthly cost of private mortgage insurance (PMI) if applicable. PMI is typically required if your down payment is less than 20% of the purchase price. If you don't have PMI, use 0.000% here.
- **Drop PMI LTV** - Enter the loan-to-value (LTV) ratio at which PMI will be dropped. This is the point at which your equity in the property is high enough that PMI is no

longer required. If you don't have PMI, use 0.000% here.

Monthly Income

Accurately estimating your monthly income is critical for assessing the profitability of your real estate investment. This section will guide you through the necessary inputs for calculating your expected monthly income from the property, including rent and any additional sources of income.

- **Monthly Rent** - Enter the amount of rent you expect to receive from tenants each month. If you don't know how to determine what rent is on a property you're considering, you might want to check out our book on *How to Determine Rent Comps*.
- **Monthly Other Income** - Enter any additional monthly income from the property, such as parking fees, laundry services, or storage rentals.

Annual Expenses

Understanding and accurately estimating annual expenses is crucial for analyzing the financial viability of a real estate investment. This section will guide you through the various costs associated with owning and maintaining a property, from vacancy rates to property taxes and insurance. By thoroughly accounting for each of these expenses, you can better predict your investment's profitability and make more informed decisions.

- **Vacancy Rate** - Enter the percentage of time the property is expected to be vacant each year.
- **Property Taxes** - Enter the annual property tax amount you will pay for owning the property.
- **Property Insurance** - Enter the annual cost of insuring the property.
- **HOA Dues** - Enter the annual homeowner association fees, if applicable.
- **Utilities** - Enter the annual cost of utilities that you will pay as the property owner.
- **Other Expenses 1 and 2** - Enter any other annual expenses not covered in the previous categories.
- **Maintenance** - Enter the annual cost of maintaining the property, including repairs and routine upkeep.
- **CapEx** - Enter the annual amount set aside for capital expenditures. Consider our book and spreadsheet on CapEx for more guidance.
- **Management** - Enter the annual cost of property management services, if applicable.

Depreciation Details

Depreciation Is a critical aspect of real estate investment analysis, as it allows you to account for the gradual reduction in the value of your property over time. Properly calculating and understanding depreciation can provide significant tax benefits and improve the overall financial picture of your investment. This section will guide you through the necessary inputs for determining depreciation, including land value, property type, and your effective income tax rate. By accurately inputting these details, you can optimize your investment strategy and maximize potential returns.

- **Land Value** - Enter the percent of the property that represents the value of the land. This value is used to calculate depreciation.
- **Property Type (C or R)** - Indicate whether the property is classified as commercial (C) or residential (R). This affects the depreciation schedule.
- **Effective Income Tax Rate** - Enter your effective income tax rate. This rate is used to estimate the tax benefits of depreciation.

Overrides

The spreadsheet is designed to be user-friendly on the Dashboard, while offering extensive functionality in the Overrides section. This dual approach ensures that users can easily navigate and input basic data, but also have access to more advanced features when needed.

In the Overrides tab, you have the ability to:

- **Modify any other inputs** - Adjust various parameters to suit your specific needs and scenarios.
- **Perform custom calculations** - Create and implement your own unique calculations to gain deeper insights into your investments.

- **View intermediate calculations** - Access detailed breakdowns of the calculations that drive the final results, providing transparency and better understanding.
- **Analyze performance over an extended period** - The spreadsheet allows you to conduct analysis through up to 40 years, enabling long-term strategic planning.
- **Track investment performance** - Use the Overrides tab to monitor how your investment evolves over time, making it easier to adjust your strategy as needed.

This comprehensive functionality ensures that the spreadsheet is not only a powerful tool for initial analysis but also a valuable resource for ongoing management and optimization of your real estate investments.

Dashboard

The Dashboard section provides a comprehensive overview of your real estate investment's key metrics and financial performance.

Here, you can quickly assess your monthly cash flow, return on investment (ROI), internal rate of return (IRR), and other critical indicators.

The Dashboard is designed to offer a user-friendly summary of your investment, allowing you to make informed decisions and track your progress over time.

Of course, you can dig into the Overrides tab for a ridiculous amount of additional detail.

Monthly Cash Flow - Year 1

This chart displays the Monthly Cash Flow, *Cash Flow from Depreciation*™, and the combined total, referred to as *True Cash Flow*™.

Understanding these metrics is crucial as they provide a comprehensive view of your investment's financial health.

- Monthly Cash Flow shows the actual cash inflow and outflow.
- *Cash Flow from Depreciation*™ accounts for tax benefits derived from property depreciation.
- *True Cash Flow*™ combines these figures, offering a more accurate representation of your investment's profitability.

Return in Dollars - Year 1

This chart displays the estimated dollars earned from your real estate investment over the first year, including Appreciation, Cash Flow, *Cash Flow from Depreciation*™, and Debt Paydown.

Understanding these metrics provides a holistic view of your investment's performance:

- **Appreciation** - Reflects the increase in property value over the year.
- **Cash Flow** - Shows the actual cash inflow and outflow.
- ***Cash Flow from Depreciation***™ - Accounts for tax benefits derived from property depreciation.

- **Debt Paydown** - Indicates the amount of principal paid down on your mortgage over the year.

Additionally, the chart includes earnings on reserves:

- **6 Months of Reserves in Savings** - Illustrates the interest earned if you set aside 6 months of reserves in a savings account.
- **Most of 12 Months of Reserves in Another Investment** - Shows the potential earnings if most of 12 months of reserves are invested in another investment vehicle like the stock market.

These combined figures provide a comprehensive representation of your investment's profitability and financial health over the first year.

You can see the totals at the bottom of the chart.

Return on Investment - Year 1

This chart displays the return on investment (ROI) from your real estate investment over the first year, including Appreciation, Cash Flow, *Cash Flow from Depreciation*™, and Debt Paydown.

Understanding these metrics provides a holistic view of your investment's performance:

- **Appreciation** - Reflects the increase in property value over the year divided by the total amount invested (and reserves where applicable).

- **Cash Flow** - Shows the actual cash inflow and outflow divided by the total amount invested (and reserves where applicable).
- *Cash Flow from Depreciation*™ - Accounts for tax benefits derived from property depreciation divided by the total amount invested (and reserves where applicable).
- **Debt Paydown** - Indicates the amount of principal paid down on your mortgage over the year divided by the total amount invested (and reserves where applicable).

Additionally, the chart includes ROI on reserves:

- **6 Months of Reserves in Savings** - Illustrates the interest earned if you set aside 6 months of reserves in a savings account, divided by the total amount invested plus 6 months of reserves.
- **Most of 12 Months of Reserves in Another Investment** - Shows the potential earnings if most of 12 months of reserves are invested in another investment vehicle like the stock market, divided by the total amount invested plus 12 months of reserves.

These combined figures provide a comprehensive representation of your investment's profitability and financial health over the first year in terms of ROI.

You can see the totals at the bottom of the chart.

Returns if Sold (ROI and IRR)

This chart illustrates the return on investment if you sold the property each year for the first 20 years. It includes three key metrics:

- **Simple Annualized Return on Investment** - This metric shows the average annual return on your investment, calculated by dividing the total return by the number of years you held the property.
- **Compound Annualized Return on Investment** - This metric accounts for the compounding effect, showing the average annual return on your investment when considering the reinvestment of earnings.
- **Internal Rate of Return (IRR)** - This metric represents the annualized rate of return that makes the net present value (NPV) of all cash flows (both inflows and outflows) from the investment equal to zero.

These metrics provide a comprehensive view of the financial performance of your investment over time, helping you to understand the potential long-term profitability and compare it with other investment opportunities.

Cash on Cash ROI & Cap Rate - Years 1-5

This chart displays the Cash on Cash Return on Investment (ROI) and the Capitalization Rate (Cap Rate) for the property over the first 5 years.

Understanding these metrics provides a comprehensive view of your investment's performance:

- **Cash on Cash ROI** - This metric shows the annual return on your investment based on the actual cash invested. It is calculated by dividing the annual pre-tax cash flow by the total cash invested.
- **Cap Rate** - This metric represents the annual return on the property based on its current market value. It is calculated by dividing the net operating income (NOI) by the property's current market value.

By understanding these metrics, you can gauge the effectiveness and profitability of your investment, enabling you to make well-informed decisions and evaluate it against other potential investment opportunities.

Return on True Net Equity™

This chart shows you the returns you're earning from Appreciation, Cash Flow, *Cash Flow from Depreciation*™, and Debt Paydown divided by the equity minus the costs to access that equity with a sale (what we call True Net Equity™). It shows the first 20 years. It also shows the total of all four areas of return.

Understanding these metrics is crucial for assessing the true profitability of your real estate investment:

- **Appreciation** - Reflects the increase in property value over the year.
- **Cash Flow** - Shows the actual cash inflow and outflow.

- *Cash Flow from Depreciation*™ - Accounts for tax benefits derived from property depreciation.
- **Debt Paydown** - Indicates the amount of principal paid down on your mortgage over the year.

By dividing these returns by the True Net Equity™, you get a more accurate representation of your investment's performance, considering the costs to access the equity. This comprehensive view helps in making informed decisions and comparing the potential returns of different investments.

For more information on True Net Equity™ consider checking out our books about that:

- Should I Sell My Rental My Rental Property?
- Should I Sell My Refinance My Rental Property?

Annual Key Metrics - Year 1

This chart displays the financial performance of your real estate investment in terms of Gross Potential Income (GPI), Gross Operating Income (GOI), Operating Expenses (OpEx), and Net Operating Income (NOI) for the first year.

Understanding these metrics provides a comprehensive view of your investment's revenue and profitability:

- **Gross Potential Income (GPI)** - This metric represents the total income the property could generate if it were fully rented and all units were occupied at market rent rates, without accounting for any vacancies or losses.

- **Gross Operating Income (GOI)** - This metric reflects the actual income received from the property, including rent and other income sources, after accounting for vacancies and any collection losses.
- **Operating Expenses (OpEx)** - These are the costs associated with maintaining and managing the property, excluding mortgage payments and capital expenditures.
- **Net Operating Income (NOI)** - This metric is calculated by subtracting the operating expenses from the Gross Operating Income. It represents the income generated by the property after all operating expenses have been deducted.

By understanding these metrics, you can better assess the financial health and profitability of your real estate investment, helping you make more strategic decisions and compare it with other investment opportunities.

Annual Non-Loan Expenses - Year 1

This chart displays the financial performance of your real estate investment by itemizing all the non-loan expenses for the first year. Understanding these metrics provides a comprehensive view of your property's operational costs, which are crucial for accurate financial analysis and planning:

- **Vacancy Rate** - The percentage of time the property is expected to be vacant each year.

- **Property Taxes** - The annual amount paid for property taxes.
- **Property Insurance** - The cost of insuring the property for the year.
- **HOA Dues** - Annual homeowner association fees, if applicable.
- **Utilities** - The total annual cost of utilities paid by the property owner.
- **Other Expenses 1 and 2** - Any additional annual expenses not covered in the previous categories.
- **Maintenance** - The annual expense for maintaining the property, including routine repairs and upkeep.
- **CapEx** - The annual amount set aside for capital expenditures, such as major repairs or replacements.
- **Management Fees** - The cost of property management services, if utilized.

By breaking down these non-loan expenses, this chart helps you understand the total operational costs associated with your property, enabling you to better manage your investment and forecast its financial performance.

Equities and Cost-To-Access

This chart displays the equity in your real estate deal each year for the first 20 years, focusing on two key metrics: *True Net Equity*™ and Cash-Out Refi Equity.

- ***True Net Equity*™** - This is the equity minus the costs to access it through a sale. It shows the real profit after considering selling costs.

- **Cash-Out Refi Equity** - This is the equity available if you refinance the property. It helps you understand the potential funds available through refinancing.
- **Cost-To-Access Equity Percentages** - The chart also shows the costs (as a percentage of the equity) associated with accessing each type of equity. This provides insight into the expenses involved.

Understanding these metrics is crucial for knowing how much money you could pull out of the investment over time and the cost to access that equity if you choose to do so.

Trademarks: The World's Greatest Real Estate Deal Analysis Spreadsheet™, Cash Flow from Depreciation™, True Cash Flow, True Net Equity™, and Nomad™ are trademarks of James Orr and/or Real Estate Financial Planner LLC. All rights reserved.

94 Ways to Improve Cash Flow on Rental Properties

You might find yourself in a real estate market where:

- Property prices are high—possibly even soaring,
- Mortgage interest rates are elevated—maybe significantly so,
- Yet rents, despite any increases, haven't risen enough to offset these higher prices and rates.

Instead of the steady stream of cash flow you anticipated, you may be seeing just a trickle.

As a real estate broker, I developed the *Lowest Monthly Payment Guarantee*™ for my clients. This comprehensive checklist—backed by a *cash-in-your-pocket guarantee*—promised to uncover every possible way to reduce and minimize their monthly payments when purchasing a property.

For my real estate investor clients, I went a step further and created the *Maximum Cash Flow Guarantee*™. This second checklist—also backed by a *cash-in-your-pocket guarantee*—was designed to help them identify every possible way to increase and maximize the income generated from their rental properties.

Simply put, cash flow is the difference between income and expenses.

By maximizing income and minimizing expenses on a rental property, you can significantly boost your cash flow.

Below, you'll find an abridged version of these two checklists—combined into one—designed to help you maximize cash flow on your rental properties.

For your convenience, I've organized the strategies into seven distinct stages of the real estate investing process.

7 Distinct Real Estate Investing Stages for Improving Cash Flow

The real estate investing process can be broken down into seven distinct stages, each offering unique opportunities to improve cash flow:

1. **Searching for Properties** - Strategies to enhance cash flow while you're searching for a property to buy.

2. **Financing the Property** - Tactics to maximize cash flow when securing financing for the property you're purchasing.

3. **Improving the Real Estate Investing Strategy** - Different real estate investing strategies produce varying levels of cash flow. Here, you'll find strategies tailored to the specific investing approach you choose once you've acquired the property.

4. **Improving the Property** - Cash flow enhancement strategies based on making physical improvements to the property itself.

5. **Marketing the Property for Rent** - Techniques to boost cash flow during the process of marketing your property to prospective tenants.

6. **While Owning the Property** - Strategies you can implement at any time during ownership to optimize cash flow.

7. **While Renting the Property** - Methods to improve cash flow while actively renting out the property.

While applying strategies from each stage will maximize your cash flow, you can also focus on the stage you're currently in. Implement what you can now, and revisit these strategies regularly to continuously improve—aim for just a 1% improvement each month.

Searching for Properties

Here are the cash flow improving strategies to implement while searching for a property to buy.

- **Agent Selection** - Choosing the right real estate agent can have a significant impact on your investment's cash flow. Some agents offer lower commissions or commission rebates. This money can appear as improved cash flow in the first year or use the money to buy down your mortgage interest rate and get improved cash flow for the life of the loan.
- **Lock/Float** - When securing financing for a property, interest rates can fluctuate. Locking in an interest rate early can protect you from rising rates during the closing process, while floating allows you to benefit from potential rate drops. This decision can directly influence your cash flow by affecting your monthly mortgage payments. This is especially important when buying properties that have extended under contract periods like when buying new construction.
- **Search for Less Expensive Properties** - Lower-priced properties often come with smaller mortgage payments, which can improve cash flow if you're able to get the same rent as their more expensive alternatives. For every $10,000 less expensive the property, you save approximately $50 per month (when mortgage rates are in the 5% range). Some lower priced prices will have commensurately lower rents. Analyze each deal carefully to ensure that the overall Income and expenses align to boost your cash flow.
- **Search for Pretty Properties** - Consider purchasing properties that are already in good condition and don't require significant fix-up costs. By doing so, you can allocate funds that would have been used for repairs to

increase your down payment or buy down the interest rate, both of which can lead to better cash flow.

- **Search for Seller Concessions** - Seller concessions are contributions from the seller to help cover your closing costs. By negotiating for these concessions, you can reduce your out-of-pocket expenses or even use them to buy down your mortgage interest rate, both of which enhance cash flow. Consider searching for properties that are offering seller concessions.
- **Search for Creative Financing** - Creative financing can offer more favorable terms than traditional loans, directly impacting your cash flow. Here are several types of creative financing to consider:

  o **Search for Owner Financing** - Owner financing involves the seller acting as the lender, which can lead to better terms than a traditional bank loan. This can reduce your monthly payments and improve cash flow. We define owner financing as when the seller does not have a mortgage; if they have a mortgage that's wrap financing or buying the property subject to their existing mortgage which we will cover next.

  o **Search for Wrap Financing** - In wrap financing, you agree to pay the seller a monthly amount that "wraps" around their existing mortgage. The seller keeps their original mortgage in place and continues making payments to their lender. You, in turn, make payments to the seller that cover both the existing mortgage and any additional amount you've agreed upon. This can result in a lower overall interest rate compared to obtaining new financing, which can improve your cash flow. Wrap financing also gives the seller the protection of foreclosure rights if you fail to make payments.

- **Search for Subject To**- In a "subject to" arrangement, you take ownership of the property while the seller's original mortgage stays in place. Instead of wrapping a new loan around the old one, you take over making payments directly to the lender on the seller's existing loan. The loan remains in the seller's name, but you're responsible for the payments. You're not formally accountable to the lender—it's not on your credit report—but you are responsible to the seller as per your agreement. This can be advantageous if the seller's mortgage has a lower interest rate than what's currently available. Like wrap financing, this can significantly reduce your mortgage expenses and boost cash flow. However, "subject to" financing typically doesn't offer the seller the same foreclosure protections as wrap financing does.

- **Search for Assumable Loans** - Some loans can be formally transferred from the seller to the buyer, keeping the original interest rate intact. If the seller's loan has a lower interest rate, assuming the loan can significantly boost your cash flow. Since most loan assumptions are for owner-occupant borrowers this strategy likely only applies to those utilizing an owner-occupant investing strategy like house hacking or Nomad™.

- **Search for Rent-To-Own Properties** - Rent-to-own agreements allow you to lease a property with the option to purchase it later. These arrangements can offer lower initial payments and more flexible terms, which may improve your cash flow compared to traditional financing.

- **Search for Agreements for Deed** - Also called bond for deed, contract for deed, or installment land contracts, these arrangements let you pay the seller directly over time. You get the deed after fulfilling the contract. This can lead to lower payments and improved cash flow while you're repaying.

- **Search for Seller Financing** - Seller financing typically involves the seller offering a loan to cover a portion of the purchase price, often as a second mortgage or "carryback" loan. In this scenario, you would secure the primary mortgage from a traditional lender, and the seller finances the remaining balance. For example, if you purchase a property for $200,000, you might get a $160,000 loan from a bank, with the seller providing a $40,000 loan. This setup can result in more favorable terms, such as lower interest rates or flexible payment schedules, improving your overall cash flow. Unlike owner financing, where the seller finances the entire purchase, seller financing usually complements other financing sources, reducing the need for a larger bank loan.

Once you've found a promising property using the strategies above, the next step is to optimize your financing to further enhance your cash flow. Let's explore the various ways you can improve your cash flow during the financing stage of your real estate investment.

Financing the Property

Here are the cash flow improving strategies to implement while financing the property you're buying.

Before Getting Loan

Here are a few strategies to improve cash flow to use before getting your loan.

- **Lender Selection** - Shop around for lenders to find one that offers better interest rates, lower fees, or more favorable terms. Different lenders have varying costs and requirements, so comparing multiple options on the same day can ensure you get the best deal, improving your overall cash flow.
- **Select by Closing Costs** - Some loans come with higher closing costs than others. By selecting a loan with lower closing costs, especially if you plan to finance these costs, you can reduce the amount you need to borrow, leading to better cash flow due to lower monthly payments.
- **Lock/Float** - Decide whether to lock in your interest rate early to protect against potential rate increases before closing, or to float and take advantage of possible rate decreases. Locking your rate provides security, while floating offers flexibility, both of which can impact your cash flow depending on market conditions.

- **Offer Less** - Negotiating a lower purchase price directly reduces the amount you need to finance, leading to lower monthly mortgage payments. This strategy can also leave more of your resources available for other cash flow improvement tactics.

Pay Upfront Instead of Financing

Here are some strategies for improving cash flow that deal with opting to pay fees upfront instead of financing them.

- **Seller Concessions** - Negotiate for the seller to cover some of your closing costs or to provide credits that can be used to buy down your mortgage interest rate. This is almost certainly required to be done at the time you make your offer and not after your offer is accepted. This reduces your upfront cash outlay and can lower your monthly mortgage payments, thereby improving cash flow.
- **Pay Closing Costs** - Paying your closing costs upfront instead of rolling them into your mortgage can reduce the amount you borrow, lowering your monthly payments and improving cash flow over the life of the loan.
- **Pre-Pay PMI** - If you're required to pay Private Mortgage Insurance (PMI), consider pre-paying it in a lump sum rather than monthly. This reduces your ongoing monthly expenses, leading to better cash flow.
- **Staggered Rate** - Opt for a staggered interest rate loan, where the interest rate is lower in the initial years

and increases over time. This can provide you with better cash flow during the early years of the loan when you may need it most.

- **Buy Down Rate** - Pay upfront to lower your mortgage interest rate for the life of the loan. A lower interest rate means a lower monthly payment, which can significantly improve your cash flow over time. For long-term buy and hold real estate investors—especially if you find yourself in a low mortgage interest rate environment—this can be an amazing strategy.

Change/Improve Borrower(s)

These strategies for improving cash flow relate to changing or improving the borrower on the loan.

- **Credit Score** - Improving your credit score can help you secure a lower interest rate and reduce your PMI rate. Both of these improvements lead to lower monthly payments and better cash flow.
- **Add Borrower** - Adding a co-borrower with a strong credit profile to your loan can help you qualify for a better interest rate and lower PMI, both of which can enhance your cash flow.
- **Remove Borrower** - If one borrower has a weaker credit profile, removing them from the loan might result in a better interest rate. This can lead to lower monthly payments and improved cash flow.
- **Loan Partner** - Partnering with someone who has a strong financial profile can help you secure better loan

terms, including lower interest rates and more favorable conditions, which ultimately enhance your cash flow.

Relationship With Lender

These cash flow improving strategies are based on your relationship with the lender or lending institution.

- **Auto Pay Loan** - Setting up automatic payments can sometimes qualify you for a slight reduction in your interest rate, directly improving your cash flow by lowering your monthly mortgage payment. It may show up also as a penalty to the interest rate if you don't use autopay for the mortgage.
- **Additional Accounts** - Maintaining additional accounts or depositing more funds with your lender might earn you a small interest rate reduction, leading to improved cash flow through lower monthly payments. This is more common with commercial loans and relationship banking.

Change Amortization

These strategies to improve your cash flow deal with changing the amortization schedule of the financing you're getting.

- **Interest Only** - An interest-only loan allows you to pay only the interest for a certain period, which significantly reduces your monthly payments. This can boost your cash flow in the short term, though it comes with long-term risks since the principal remains unpaid. You'll need to have a solid plan to deal with the loan balance when the ballon payment date arrives.

- **Negative Amortization** - A negative amortizing loan allows you to pay less than the interest due, causing the loan balance to increase over time. This lowers your initial payments and improves short-term cash flow but increases your debt over time.
- **Rate from Loan Term** - Shortening the loan term (e.g., switching from a 30-year to a 15-year mortgage) can lower your interest rate. However, this typically increases your monthly payments, so it's more about long-term savings than immediate cash flow improvement.
- **Loan Term** - Extending the loan term (e.g., from 30 to 40 years) reduces the monthly payment amount, which can improve your cash flow. However, this means you'll pay more interest over the life of the loan.

Loan Terms

These cash flow improving strategies deal with the terms (details) of the loan itself.

- **Amount Borrowed** - Putting more money down reduces the amount you need to borrow, leading to lower monthly payments. This can improve your cash flow, though it also means tying up more capital in the property.

- **Loan-To-Value** - A lower loan-to-value (LTV) ratio, achieved by making a larger down payment, often results in a better interest rate. This lowers your monthly payments and improves cash flow. Not only can putting more down improve your LTV and give you a better interest rate, but it might also reduce your Private Mortgage Insurance (PMI) payment since that's part of the calculation for determining PMI amounts.
- **Adjustable Rate** - An adjustable-rate mortgage (ARM) typically starts with a lower interest rate than a fixed-rate mortgage. This can enhance your cash flow in the initial years, though the rate—and your payments—can increase later.

Private Mortgage Insurance (PMI)

These strategies to improve cash flow deal primarily with Private Mortgage Insurance (PMI).

What is PMI? The lender would prefer you put at least 20% down to finance a property. With 20% down they feel comfortable enough that if you don't pay as agreed they will be able to foreclose, sell the property and get all their money back after the expenses of foreclosure and sale.

You insist on putting less than 20% down.

They may reluctantly agree, but they may charge you a higher interest rate because it is a riskier loan to them. And, additionally, they may insist that you pay a third-party insurance company a fee that insures them in case you default and they're unable to foreclose and sell the property to recoup their entire investment. This third-party insurance company is Private Mortgage Insurance.

It is insurance you pay for to protect the lender in case you default on the loan.

- **Eliminate PMI** - If you can put down at least 20% of the purchase price, you can avoid PMI altogether, significantly reducing your monthly mortgage expenses and improving your cash flow.
- **Pre-Pay PMI** - Paying PMI in a lump sum upfront instead of monthly can reduce your ongoing costs, leading to better cash flow throughout the loan term.
- **Improve Credit** - Enhancing your credit score can help you secure a lower PMI rate or even eliminate PMI altogether if your LTV ratio improves, both of which contribute to better cash flow.
- **Add Borrowers** - Added a borrower to your loan typically reduces PMI and therefore improves cash flow.

Other Properties

These cash flow improving strategies rely on tapping into other properties you own.

Some of these strategies deal with making sure your cash flow is optimized for your entire portfolio (including these other properties) and not specifically to a new property you're buying.

- **Cash Out Refi to Buy/Refi** - Consider doing a cash-out refinance on another property to use the proceeds for purchasing or refinancing your current property. This can result in better overall financing terms and improved cash flow.
- **Cash Out Refi for Larger Down Payment** - If putting more down on your current property will secure a better interest rate or eliminate PMI, consider using funds from a cash-out refinance on another property. This can lower your monthly payments and improve cash flow.
- **Rate and Term Before Acquisition** - Before purchasing a new property, consider refinancing your existing properties to better terms. As you own more properties the complexity of refinancing increases significantly. Consider this a reminder to consider this before each new purchase and to make any changes to other properties now before you add a new property that further limits what you can do. This can also improve the overall cash flow on your portfolio and might also allow you to qualify for better financing on the new purchase.

Non-Traditional Financing

These are some non-traditional financing strategies for improving cash flow you might want to consider.

- **Pay Cash** - If you have sufficient funds, paying cash for a property eliminates the need for financing altogether,

90

which maximizes cash flow by removing monthly mortgage payments.

- **Private Financing** - Secure a loan from family or friends (private lenders) who might offer more favorable terms than traditional banks. This can lead to lower monthly payments and improved cash flow.
- **Creative Financing** - Explore options like owner financing, wrap financing, agreement for deed, lease-options, or subject to, where the seller might offer better terms than traditional lenders. These strategies can lower your mortgage payments and enhance cash flow.
- **Assumable Loan** - If the seller's existing loan has a lower interest rate than current market rates, assuming their loan can be a great way to secure better financing terms, leading to improved cash flow. This is more likely for owner-occupant loans, so this is probably limited to owner-occupant investing strategies like house hacking or Nomad™.

While optimizing your financing is crucial for improving cash flow, it's equally important to consider how your chosen real estate investing strategy can impact your returns. Let's now explore various strategies that can enhance your cash flow by refining your overall investment approach.

Improving the Real Estate Investing Strategy

Here are the cash flow improving strategies based on improving the real estate investing strategy you're opting to utilize.

- **Term** - Adjusting the duration of your lease can significantly impact your cash flow. Shorter-term rentals, such as daily, weekly, or monthly leases, often command higher rents compared to yearly leases. However, shorter terms can also lead to increased expenses, including higher vacancy rates, more frequent marketing, and potentially higher management and maintenance costs. Offering different terms, such as furnished vs. unfurnished rentals, can also cater to various market segments, like vacation rentals or boarding houses, providing opportunities to maximize income.

- **Lease-Option** - Lease-option strategies, including variations like rent-to-own (like lease-purchases and lease-options), can dramatically improve cash flow, particularly in markets where buying is significantly more expensive than renting. These arrangements typically involve collecting a non-refundable purchase deposit/option fee, which can—mathematically—appear to add hundreds of dollars per month to your cash flow. Additionally, tenants in lease-option agreements often treat the property with more care, reducing maintenance, vacancy, and management costs. This strategy is a form of our *Deal Alchemy*™, where you trade future appreciation returns for immediate cash flow.

- **Niche** - Specializing in a specific rental market can allow you to charge premium rents by catering to unique needs. For example, you might focus on corporate rentals, traveling nurses, or student housing. By understanding and addressing the specific requirements of your niche audience, such as providing furnished units for corporate rentals or flexible leases for students, you can add value that justifies higher rental rates. The key is to determine what additional services or amenities you can offer that will attract your target market and what premium you can reasonably charge for those services.

The following cash flow improving strategies are really just variations of house hacking where you're renting out part of the property you're living in for income and to improve cash flow. However, you could utilize these strategies even when you're not living in the property.

- **Roommates** - Renting out individual bedrooms in a single-family home, or additional units in a duplex, triplex, or fourplex, can significantly increase your cash flow. This is a common house hacking strategy where you live in one part of the property and rent out the rest. For example, you might rent out spare bedrooms in your own home or lease the other units in a multi-family property. This approach allows you to maximize the rental income from a single property by utilizing every available space.

- **Rent by Bed/Bedroom** - Some properties, particularly those near colleges or universities, may lend themselves well to renting by the bedroom or even by the bed. This strategy works particularly well with student housing, where multiple tenants share a single property. By renting out each bedroom or bed individually, you can often achieve a higher overall rent compared to leasing the entire property to a single tenant.
- **Rent by Parts** - Renting out different parts of a property, such as non-conforming units in a duplex, triplex, or fourplex, can be a lucrative strategy. It's essential to check local occupancy laws to ensure compliance. This strategy can also include more unconventional setups, such as renting out RV parking spaces, tiny homes, garages, or storage units on the property. These spaces don't have to be residential; they can be rented for commercial or recreational purposes, such as storage or use of shared community amenities like a pool or recreational center.

While optimizing your real estate investing strategy can significantly boost cash flow, another powerful approach is to enhance the property itself. By making strategic improvements and modifications to your rental property, you can potentially increase its value and appeal, leading to higher rental income and improved cash flow. Let's explore some effective strategies for improving cash flow through property enhancements.

Improving the Property

Here are the cash flow improving strategies based on making improvements to the property.

- **Subdivide** - Consider subdividing your property into multiple units to increase rental income. For example, you could rent the upstairs and downstairs separately, offering tenants more privacy while still sharing common areas like heating, cooling, mail, laundry, and possibly even the kitchen or living areas. This isn't the same as converting the property into a formal duplex or triplex; instead, it's more about creating a roommate-like situation with more separation. This setup allows you to comply with local roommate laws and zoning requirements while potentially charging higher rents, as tenants may feel like they have their own space.

- **Upgrade Property** - Enhancing your property's curb appeal and overall condition can justify charging higher rents. Improvements could include landscaping, painting, adding or improving shutters, lawn care, updating the mailbox, property address numbers, or exterior lighting. These upgrades can attract higher-paying tenants and increase the property's value. This approach is also common in value-add strategies or the BRRRR (Buy, Rehab, Rent, Refinance, Repeat) method, where the goal is to improve the property to increase its rent and overall profitability.

- **Solar** - Installing solar panels and including the cost of electricity in the base rent can make your property more attractive to tenants who value energy efficiency, potentially allowing you to charge higher rents. However, you should be cautious about the legal implications of charging for utilities, as this can sometimes enter a gray area. It's advisable to consult with a local attorney to ensure compliance with utility billing regulations.

- **Furnished Rental** - Offering a furnished rental can significantly increase the rent you can charge, especially if you shift your strategy to short-term or medium-term rentals, such as vacation rentals, student rentals, or corporate housing. Furnished rentals appeal to tenants looking for convenience and are often willing to pay a premium for a move-in ready home.

- **Convert Property** - Converting a single-family property into a duplex, triplex, or fourplex can increase your rental income by creating multiple rental units within the same property. This approach is especially effective if the property is already somewhat set up for such a conversion. However, it may be cost-prohibitive or even impossible if significant structural changes are required or if zoning laws restrict such conversions. Always check with your city and county regarding zoning and licensing requirements before starting any conversion work, as this can also affect the types of loans you can secure and their terms, including the loan-to-value ratio.

- **Improvement Rent** - Charging extra rent for specific property improvements can help offset the cost of upgrades while increasing your overall rental income. For example, you might charge a tenant more for installing new carpet or a fence. While you may not be able to recoup the full cost of the improvement from a single tenant, some upgrades, like a fence, can justify higher rents with future tenants as well, allowing you to gradually recover your investment and potentially earn a return. This strategy is particularly useful for items with a long lifespan, where the cost can be spread out over multiple tenancies.

While property improvements can significantly boost your rental income, the way you market your property can be equally important for maximizing cash flow. By implementing effective marketing strategies, you can attract high-quality tenants, reduce vacancy periods, and potentially command higher rents. Let's explore some key strategies for improving cash flow through smart marketing techniques.

Marketing the Property for Rent

Here are the cash flow improving strategies to implement while you're marketing your property for rent.

- **Optimize Marketing** - Effective marketing starts with high-quality materials. Ensure that you have professional-grade photos, a 3D tour, and a video to showcase your property. These elements can significantly enhance the appeal of your listing, attracting more potential tenants. Additionally, use online marketing as well as flyers and signs strategically around the neighborhood to increase visibility. Well-designed marketing materials make your property stand out and convey a sense of professionalism that can justify higher rent and reduce vacancy periods.

- **Maximize Exposure** - To attract the right tenants, it's crucial to advertise your property across all available platforms where tenants might be searching. This includes online rental websites, social media, and community bulletin boards. Physical advertising, such as yard signs and directional signs leading to the property, can also capture the attention of local renters. By maximizing exposure, you increase the chances of filling vacancies quickly and with quality tenants.
- **Sales Skills** - Mastering sales skills is essential for renting your property at the highest possible rate and minimizing vacancy. This includes both phone skills for initial inquiries and in-person salesmanship during property tours. Being persuasive and knowledgeable helps you connect with potential tenants, address their concerns, and highlight the property's best features, ultimately leading to faster lease agreements and better tenant retention.
- **Optimize Showings** - Preparing your property for showings is a key step in securing a lease. Ensure the property is well-lit, smells pleasant, and is clean, neat, and in good repair. First impressions matter, and a well-presented property can make the difference between a potential tenant choosing your property over another. Additionally, create a sense of scarcity by scheduling back-to-back showings and mentioning this when booking appointments. This strategy can create urgency and increase interest among prospective tenants.

While effective marketing strategies can help attract tenants and maximize rental income, it's equally important to focus on optimizing your property's financial performance during ownership. Let's explore various strategies you can implement to improve cash flow throughout your tenure as a property owner.

While Owning the Property

Here are the cash flow improving strategies to implement while you own the property.

Refi/Pay Off Loan

Managing your mortgage can be one of the most effective ways to improve cash flow and overall property profitability.

- **Refi to Extend Term** - If your loan is old enough, consider refinancing to extend the loan term. This can lower your monthly payments and—if interest rates have dropped and/or your loan-to-value has improved—potentially secure a better interest rate, improving your cash flow.
- **Refi to Improve Rate** - If interest rates have dropped since you first took out your mortgage, refinancing to a lower rate can reduce your monthly payments and save you money over the life of the loan.
- **Payoff Loan** - If you have the financial means, paying off your loan in its entirety can eliminate your mortgage

payments, drastically improving your monthly cash flow and reducing financial stress.

Taxes

Property taxes are a significant expense for any property owner, and managing them effectively can save you money.

- **Correct Assessor** - Ensure that the county assessor has accurate information about your property's condition and characteristics. Correcting any inaccuracies can prevent overvaluation and keep your taxes in check.
- **Contest Tax Increases** - If your property taxes increase, consider contesting the increase. Successful challenges can lead to reduced tax bills and improved cash flow.
- **Vote** - Participate in local elections and vote on measures that affect property taxes. Being informed and voting appropriately can help control future tax increases.

Insurance

Insurance is essential for protecting your investment, but it's also an area where you can manage costs.

- **Shop Insurance Rates** - Regularly compare insurance rates from different providers to ensure you're getting the best deal. Competitive rates can lower your insurance costs without sacrificing coverage.

- **Insurance Coverage** - Review your property insurance policy to make sure you have the right level of coverage. Avoid overpaying for unnecessary coverage or underinsuring your property. It is not just about minimizing this cost while sacrificing coverage; you must make sure you minimize cost while keeping a desirable level of coverage. Sacrificing coverage is short-sighted and might significantly hurt cash flow if you ever have a claim that is you opted not to cover.
- **Insured** - Adjust your insurance policy by adding or removing people as needed to optimize your rates. This can lead to lower premiums.
- **Insurance Deductible** - Consider raising your deductible to lower your insurance premium. Taking on more risk personally can reduce your monthly insurance costs. See comments about sacrificing coverage being short-sighted above.
- **Remove PMI** - Totally different type of insurance, but if your property's equity has increased sufficiently, you may be able to remove Private Mortgage Insurance (PMI). This can significantly reduce your monthly mortgage payment.

Making Payments

How you manage your payments can also impact your overall costs.

- **Discount for Autopay** - Sign up for autopay on utilities and other bills to avoid per-bill fees. Many service providers offer small discounts or waive fees for customers who enroll in autopay.
- **Discount for Early Payments** - Some service providers, such as HOA or insurance companies, offer discounts for early payments. Paying these bills in advance can reduce your overall expenses.

Management

Whether you manage your property yourself or hire a professional, effective management is key to maintaining profitability.

- **Self-Manage** - If you choose to manage the property yourself, ensure you stay up to date with the latest laws, best practices, and compliance issues. Self-management can save on property management fees, but it often requires a significant time investment.
- **Professional Property Manager** - Shop around for a high-quality property manager who offers reasonable fees. A good property manager can maximize your rental income and minimize headaches.
- **Manage the Manager** - Even with a professional property manager, it's important to regularly review management statements for accuracy. Mistakes can happen, and catching them early can save you money.
- **Insist on Best Practices** - Ensure your property manager follows best practices, such as marketing your

property early and raising rents with each lease renewal. This proactive approach can help maximize your rental income.

Maintenance

Regular maintenance is crucial for keeping your property in good condition and minimizing vacancies.

- **Maintain Property** - Regularly maintaining your property can reduce the time it spends vacant between tenants. A well-maintained property attracts tenants quickly and reduces downtime.
- **Quality Materials** - Using quality materials for maintenance and repairs may have a higher upfront cost, but it can lower the overall cost of maintenance over time by reducing the frequency of repairs and replacements.

Depreciation

Depreciation can provide significant tax benefits, and managing it strategically can enhance your investment returns.

- **Accelerate Depreciation** - Consider accelerating depreciation on your property to maximize tax benefits in the short term. This strategy can improve your cash flow by reducing your taxable income, but it should be used with careful planning to avoid potential future tax liabilities. This can be one of the larger improvements to your cash flow.

While the strategies for improving cash flow during property ownership are crucial, it's equally important to optimize your rental income while renting it. Let's explore various techniques you can implement to enhance your cash flow during the rental phase of your investment.

While Renting the Property

Here are the cash flow improving strategies to implement while you're renting the property.

Add Services

Offering additional services can increase rental income and enhance tenant satisfaction.

- **Additional Services** - Consider offering additional services such as high-speed internet, cable, or utilities for an extra fee. Tenants often value the convenience of bundled services, making this an effective way to boost your rental income. However, be sure to check local laws, as this practice may not be permitted in some areas.
- **DFY Services** - Offer done-for-you (DFY) services such as lawn care, snow removal, or house cleaning. These services can be billed as extras, appealing to tenants who prefer convenience and are willing to pay for it.

Charge Appropriately

Setting appropriate charges can maximize your rental income while offering flexibility to tenants.

- **Bill Back** - Implement bill-back strategies for utilities or HOA services, such as charging tenants for non-potable water or other shared resources. This helps to ensure that tenants are covering their fair share of costs, improving your net income.
- **Tier Rent by Credit Score** - Adjust rent based on the tenant's credit score, with higher rent for those with lower scores. This can also apply to security deposits, where tenants with better credit pay less upfront. Check with your attorney before implementing this strategy.
- **Pet Rent** - Charge additional rent for tenants with pets. Pet rent can help cover potential wear and tear caused by pets and increase your overall rental income.

Convenience Billing

Convenience billing options can make it easier for tenants to pay rent while potentially increasing your revenue.

- **Billing Frequency** - Offer more frequent billing options, such as weekly or biweekly payments, instead of the traditional monthly schedule. This can be attractive to tenants who prefer smaller, more manageable payments but can also produce more cash flow over the same period.

- **Autopay** - Here are conflicting ideas where both options may ultimately improve cash flow. Encourage tenants to enroll in autopay by offering a discount or, conversely, charge a fee for those who do not use autopay. Autopay can reduce late payments and ensure consistent cash flow.
- **Discount On-Time Payment** - Provide a discount for tenants who pay their rent on time or early, incentivizing prompt payments and reducing the need for late payment penalties.
- **Term** - Adjust the term of rental agreements to fit different rental strategies. Consider offering daily, weekly, or short-term/vacation rentals, which can often command higher rents than traditional monthly leases.

Timing

Optimizing the timing of lease agreements and renewals can minimize vacancies and maximize rental income.

- **Notice** - Require a 60-90 day notice from tenants if they intend not to renew their lease. This provides you with ample time to market the property and secure a new tenant, reducing vacancy periods.
- **Start Early/Test Rent** - Begin marketing the property early, even before the current tenant moves out, and start with a higher rent to test the market. This strategy allows you to adjust pricing based on demand and secure the best possible rental rate.

- **Renew Peak Season** - Align lease renewal dates to end during peak rental seasons, such as spring or summer, when demand is higher. This increases the likelihood of filling the property quickly and possibly at a higher rent.

Miscellaneous

Implementing additional requirements can protect your property and reduce potential liabilities.

- **Renter's Insurance** - Require tenants to carry renter's insurance. This protects both you and the tenant in case of damage to the property or loss of personal belongings, reducing potential conflicts and liabilities.

Conclusion

This guide has explored 94 ways to improve cash flow on rental properties across seven distinct stages of your real estate investing process.

Each stage presents unique opportunities to boost your investment's financial performance, and the cumulative effect of applying these strategies can significantly increase your property's profitability.

By focusing on cash flow improvement at every stage, you can:

- Build a more resilient and profitable real estate portfolio

- Enhance property values—especially for properties where value is driven by the income they generate, such as commercial properties
- Strengthen your ability to secure favorable financing by improving loan-to-value (LTV) and debt service coverage ratios
- Optimize tax benefits
- Accelerate savings for larger down payments and quickly replenish reserves
- Increase tenant satisfaction by enhancing the tenant experience, improving retention rates, and reducing turnover costs

Remember, even small adjustments across multiple areas can compound into substantial gains in your overall returns and financial stability.

Make it a habit to regularly review and implement these strategies, tailoring them to fit your specific properties and market conditions.

With consistent effort and strategic application, you can transform your rental properties into powerful, cash-generating assets that support your long-term financial goals.

Introduction to Monte Carlo Analysis of Rental Properties

There's a problem with how we've been modeling our investments so far. It is not unique to us. Almost everyone does it wrong.

But, we're going to fix it now.

The issue is the assumptions we've been using and how the real world works.

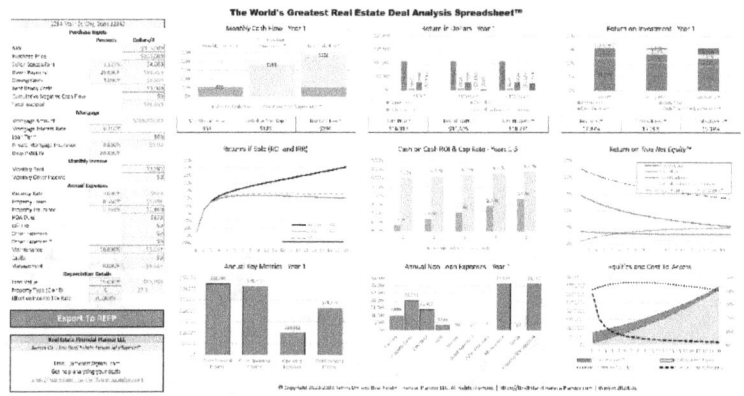

The World's Greatest Real Estate Deal Analysis Spreadsheet™

For the analysis we've been doing with *The World's Greatest Real Estate Deal Analysis Spreadsheet™* (TWGREDAS)—and any other real estate deal analysis spreadsheet—we've used static assumptions.

We might assume that property values are going up by 3% per year. Well, that's not truly a correct representation of reality.

Heck, with the overrides tab in TWGREDAS we may have said, they go up by 3% for the first 3 years and then only 2% thereafter. Better, but still not reality.

The truth is: we really don't know how much property values will go up as we hold the property. They could go up by 3%. They could go down by 3%. They could go up then down or down then up. Could be more or less than 3%. Might be 3.1% or 2.9%. Might be up or down 6% or 10%.

If we look back at history (and we do when we consider the risks of investing in real estate), we can see what property appreciation has done over the last 100 years.

Risk Matrix: Appreciation

	Severity				
	0	**1**	**2**	**3**	**4**
Likelihood	*Increase*	*Small Decline*	*Medium Decline*	*Large Decline*	*Catastrophic*
1	>10% Increase 7.7%			10-15% Decline 6.0%	>15% Decline 0.0%
2	5-10% Increase 15.0%		5-10% Decline 12.8%		
3	0-5% Increase 25.6%	0-5% Decline 34.6%			

So, to correctly model how our investment might perform, we should not use a static 3% per year—or whatever static number you believe to be true—for property appreciation.

Our crystal balls are broken. We can't accurately predict—exactly—what appreciation will be for our properties.

We can guess. Based on what has happened in the past they will average about 3% per year.

But they may:

- Increase in value by more than 10% for the year about 7.7% of the time
- Increase between 5% and 10% for the year about 15% of the time
- Increase between 0% and 5% for the year about 25.6% of the time
- Go down in value between 0% and 5% for the year about 34.6% of the time

- Go down in value between 5% and 10% for the year about 12.8% of the time
- Go down in value between 10% and 15% for the year about 6% of the time

These are based on what has happened over the last 100 years. Could the future be different? Absolutely.

But it is much more accurate than just assuming that they will be going up in value by 3% per year every year.

Not Just Property Appreciation

As you probably guessed, this isn't just an issue with property appreciation. It applies to other assumptions we have as well.

Here's a list of some of the more significant ones:

- **Property Appreciation Rate** - This is the one we've been talking about already. It is how much properties go up or down in value.
- **Rent Appreciation Rate** - This is how much rents increase or decrease with each lease renewal.
- **Inflation Rate** - Inflation reflects the overall increase in prices and the decrease in purchasing power over time. It impacts everything from the cost of goods and services to the value of money itself. In the context of your portfolio, inflation affects how much your money will be worth in the future, influencing the real returns on your investments. For instance, even if your rental

income and property values rise, high inflation could erode those gains in terms of actual purchasing power. A million dollars today isn't the same as a million dollars 50 years ago and it won't be the same as a million dollars 50 years from now.

- **Mortgage Interest Rates - Mortgage Interest Rates** - Mortgage rates fluctuate over time. The rate you secure for your current property purchase or refinance won't necessarily be the same for properties you buy in one, five, or more years from now.
- **Stock Market Rate of Return** - This is how much you're earning on money you have invested in the stock market. This also applies to other investments you might have like savings accounts, bonds, CDs, cryptocurrencies, etc.

If you really want to go to freaky town, you could also model this with changing tax rates, insurance rates, maintenance and capital expenses on the property.

Does This Even Matter?

Does this even matter and why should I care?

Let's start with a simple example of someone who invests in stocks. They don't even buy a home to live in; they rent instead.

They invest approximately 10% of their income in the stock market earning 8% per year.

Using static assumptions, we could calculate that they would be financially independent (FI) after about 53.25 years.

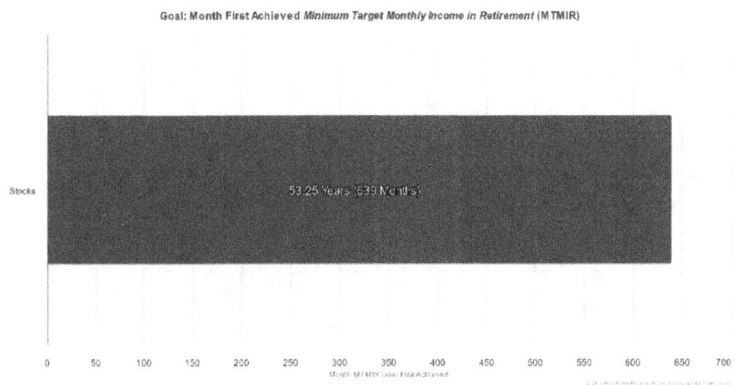

But what if we used a reasonable range of values for the return from the stock market instead of always 8% every year?

We could use a range of values that better approximates what the stock markets has done historically—still averaging about 8% for this selection of stocks.

Instead of seeing a smooth line showing their journey toward financial independence like his:

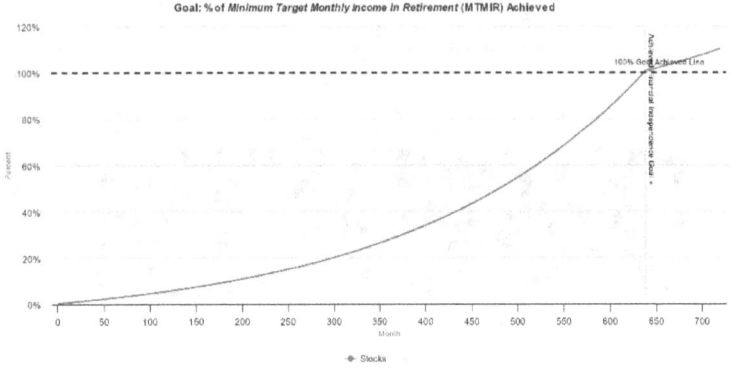

We'd instead see a less smooth line representing how the stock market returns change each month like this:

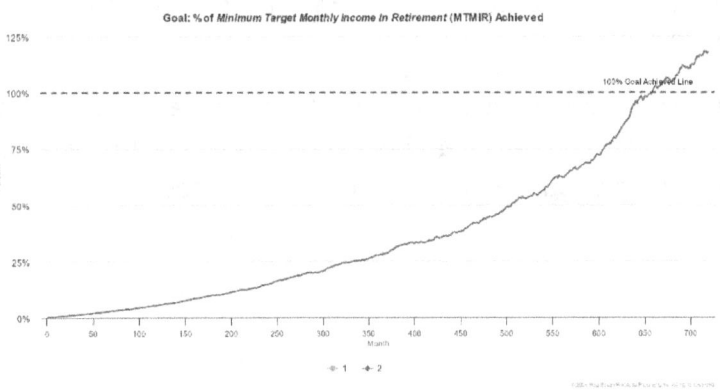

And, if we ran it 10 times, you'd see that when they actually achieve financial independence (when the line crosses the horizontal dotted line) is a little different each time.

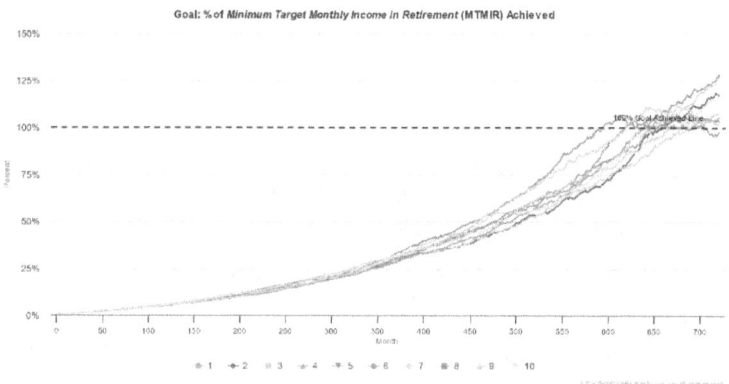

Goal: % of *Minimum Target Monthly Income in Retirement* (MTMIR) Achieved

If the stock market performs well, they're financially independent earlier. If the stock market does not perform as well, they end up being financially independent later.

If we ran this 1,000 times and summarized the results, we can see the range of when they're financially independent.

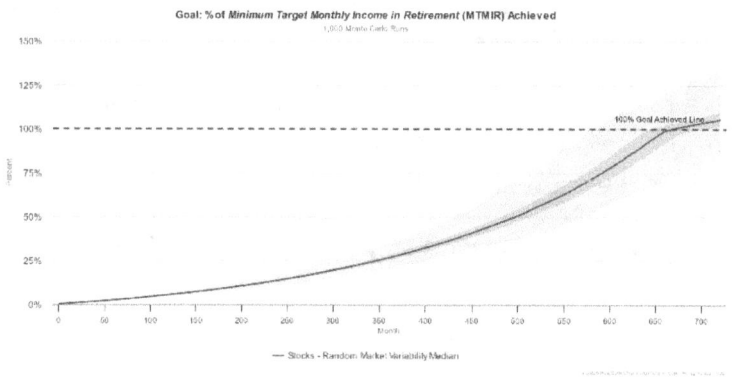

Goal: % of *Minimum Target Monthly Income in Retirement* (MTMIR) Achieved

Monte Carlo Modeling

This type of analysis is called Monte Carlo modeling.

Monte Carlo modeling is a statistical technique used to simulate multiple potential outcomes for an investment or financial scenario.

It works by:

- Running hundreds or thousands of simulations with varying input parameters
- Analyzing the range and probability of different outcomes
- Providing a more nuanced understanding of potential risks and returns

For real estate investing, Monte Carlo analysis involves varying input factors such as property appreciation rates, rent increases, mortgage interest rates, inflation, and market returns. This approach allows you to better assess the likelihood of achieving your financial goals and understand the potential risks associated with your investment strategies.

I like to call it *Alternate Universe Modeling*™ because we're consider how your investments might perform if you were living in alternate universes with different futures.

Back to our example with someone just investing in stocks.

In the chart above:

- The light blue band shows the full range of results from the very worst to the very best.
- The darker blue band in the middle shows you the middle 50% of all runs. Half of the time the results are this darker band.
- The dark link at the very center shows you the median value. Half the values are higher than this. Half the values are lower than this.

If we look at the median line we can see that half the time they're financially independent around 58 years. Half the time it is after 58 years.

It could have been as early as year 48. And, it could take longer than 60 years—when we stopped modeling for this example. In fact, only about 85% of the 1,000 runs we ran were financially independent 60 years from when they started.

We can summarize this is a different chart and show what percentage of the 1,000 runs were financially independent in each month.

That's this chart:

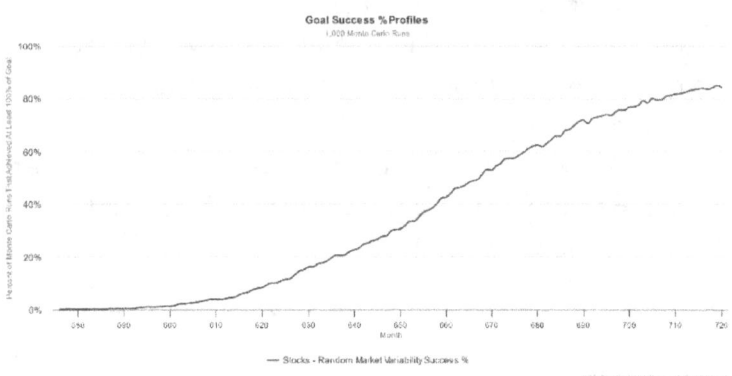

By using a range of values for things like the stock market rate of return, we get a much more nuanced understanding of what is likely to happen.

What If They Became Homeowners Instead of Renting?

Our last example they were renting a property to live in and investing in stocks.

What if they bought on owner-occupant property with 5% down to live in and invested in stocks?

If we used static assumptions they would be financially independent about 15 and half years faster:

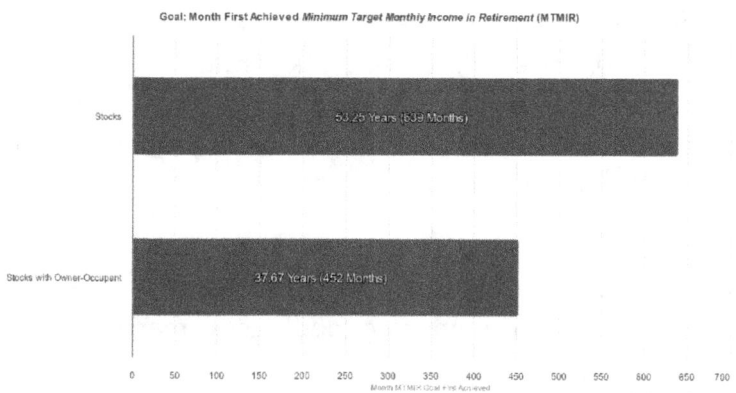

Goal: Month First Achieved *Minimum Target Monthly Income in Retirement* (MTMIR)

Part of what gets them to financial independence faster is that they end up paying off their owner-occupant property 30 years after they buy it. Without a mortgage payment the threshold for them being financially independent is a little lower.

There's a little more to this story, but I don't want to go off into the weeds here. The punchline is they achieve financial independence faster with static assumptions as you can see below:

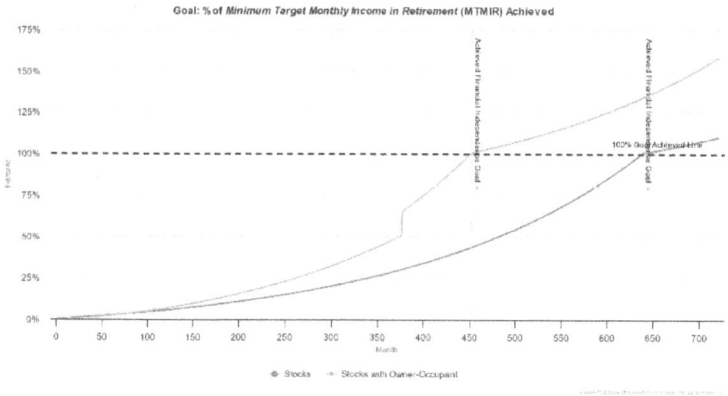

Goal: % of *Minimum Target Monthly Income in Retirement* (MTMIR) Achieved

Let's vary the property appreciation rate, mortgage interest rate, inflation rate, and stock market rate of return. If we were discussing rentals, we'd vary the rent appreciation rate as well but in this case they're not buying any rentals; we'll get to that shortly.

With variable property appreciation rates, mortgage interest rates until they lock in a 30-year fixed rate financing loan, inflation rate and stock market rate of return it looks like this:

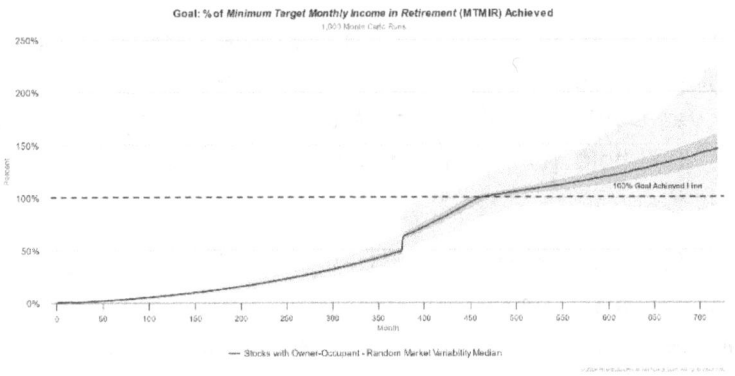

They're financially independent as early as about 33.75 years from when they start. In 99.5% of the 1,000 runs they're financially independent by the time we stop modeling at 60 years.

How does this compare to them just investing in stocks? Let's show both on one chart:

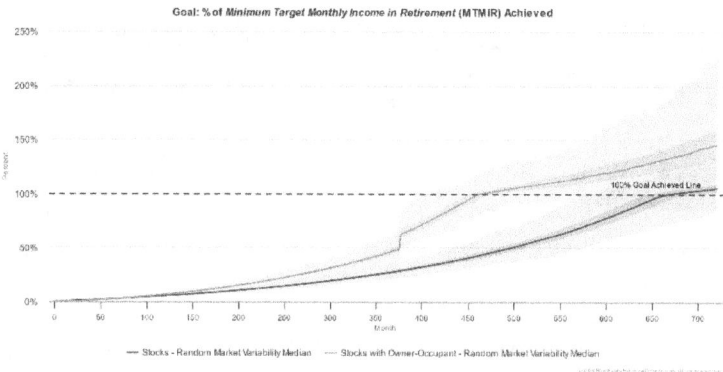

Goal: % of *Minimum Target Monthly Income in Retirement (MTMIR)* Achieved

Buying an owner-occupant property seems to make a pretty big difference.

If we just look at what percentage of the 1,000 runs they achieve financial independence, you can see that buying the owner-occupant property is more probable (higher percentage of the runs achieve it) and they're financially independent earlier (it happens more to the left on the chart).

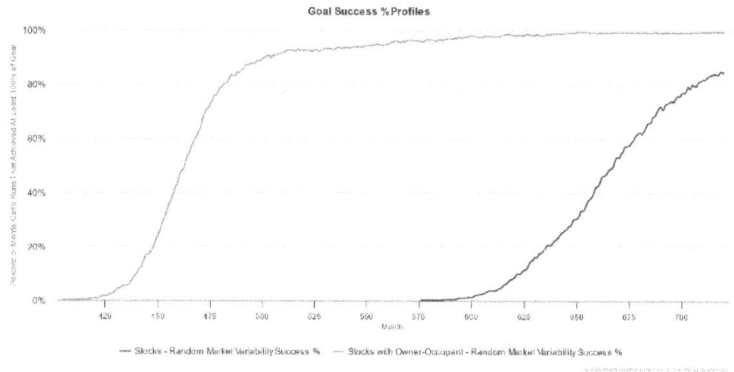

Goal Success % Profiles

Buying Rental Properties with 20% Down Payments

Let's assume, for now, that they don't buy an owner-occupant property with 5% down. Instead, they decide to buy 20% down rental properties as their primary investing strategy.

Any additional money beyond what they need for the rentals is still investing in stocks, but whenever they get enough for a 20% down payment they buy a rental property with very modest cash flow.

They're willing to buy up to ten 20% down payment rentals.

If we have **static assumptions** for property appreciation, rent appreciation, inflation, mortgage interest rates and the stock market rate of return, they might be financially independent after 31 years.

With static assumptions, that's about 18.67 years faster than just investing in stocks and about 3 years faster than buying an owner-occupant property and investing stocks:

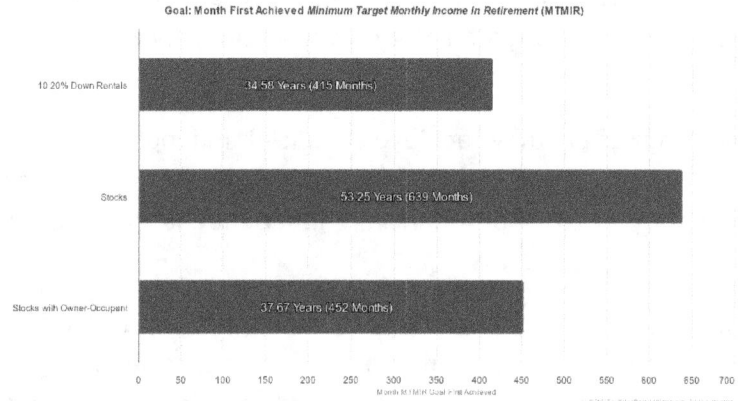

With static assumptions, they achieve financial independence faster:

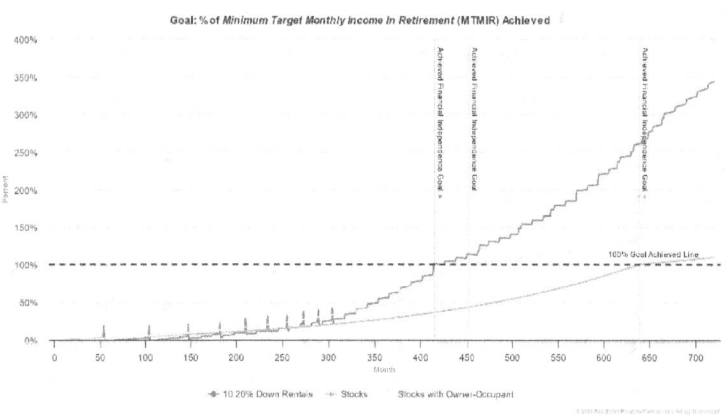

And, still looking at the chart above, they appear have a lot more income coming then just investing in stocks the longer they hold the rental properties.

In fact, they're earning about twice what they need to be financially independent about 48.5 years in. That means they're earning twice what they need to be financially independent before just investing in stocks as a renter is even earning enough for them to financially independent at all.

Not long after they achieve financial independence just investing in stocks as a renter, they're earning 3 times what they need to be financially independent with their 10 rentals.

But, this is about Monte Carlo modeling, so what if we did vary property appreciation rates, rent appreciation rates, inflation, mortgage interest rates and the stock market rate of return?

It is important to realize that because the property prices vary with each run sometimes the properties they're buying can be slightly more or less expensive. On average though, property prices are going up at about 3% per year.

Rent is similar. Rents can go up or down, but overall, rents are increasing by about 3% per year.

Mortgage interest rates started at about 8.5% for a non-owner-occupant loan without paying significant points. But, mortgage interest rates can get better—or worse—over time as they're acquiring properties. That means sometimes properties will cash flow better and sometimes they'll cash flow a little worse.

Let's look at their journey to financial independence buying ten 20% down payment rentals in the chart below:

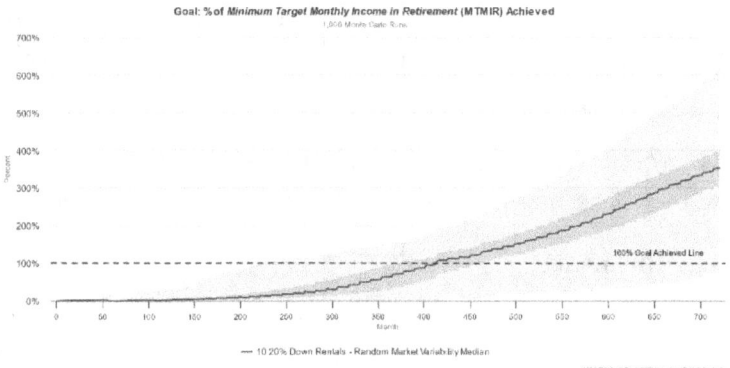

You can see there are times when the market goes in their favor (both the real estate and stock market) they achieve financial independence early. And, there are times when they still don't quite achieve it through 60 years.

How does it compare to the two previous strategies: renting and investing exclusively in stocks and buying an owner-occupant property and exclusively investing in stocks?

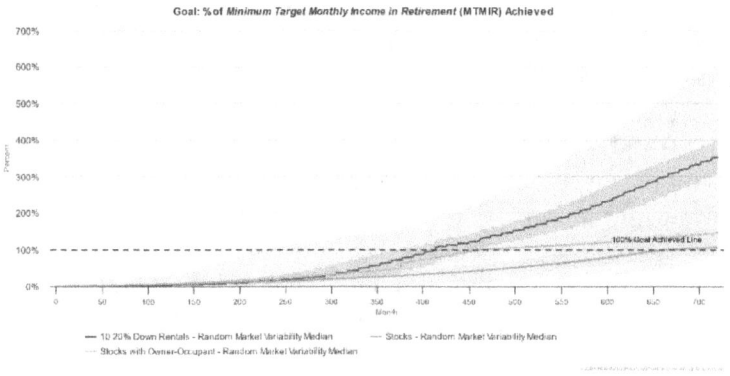

It is getting harder to see what is happening in the chart as we add additional comparisons.

We can make it easier in two different ways. First, we can look at the same chart, but turn off the shaded areas for each strategy.

This would leave just the median—or the middle-most result—where half of them are better and half are worse.

That's this chart:

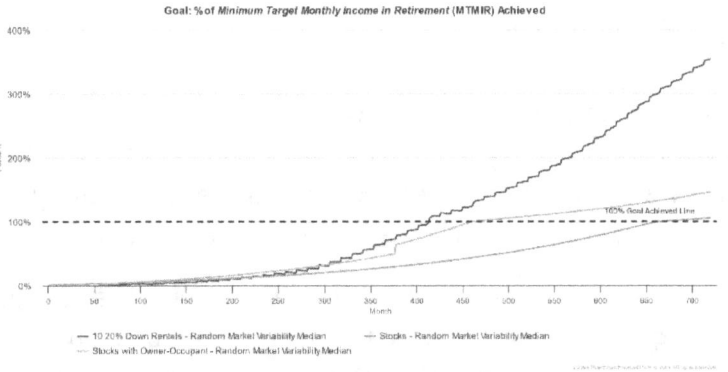

This chart doesn't show up the range of results (how early or late they achieve FI) but it does show how much more they're likely to earn by buying the rentals by what percent of their financial independence goal they're earning.

By earning a higher percentage of the amount they need to be financially independent, they're able to support a higher standard of living.

In other words, if they needed to be earning $10,000 per month passively to be considered financially independent, but their earning 200% of that—or $20,000 per month—they could live at a much higher standard of living on $20,000 per month than the $10,000 per month that they needed—at a minimum—to be considered financially independent.

The second way to make it easier to see what is happening is looking at the percentage of the 1,000 runs that achieved financial independence like we did previously.

That's this chart:

Buying ten 20% down payment rentals sees them achieving financial independence earlier (more left on the chart above) and then has a similar success rate to what they'd see if they bought an owner-occupant and invested in stocks.

Owner-Occupant, Rentals and Stocks

I think you know what's coming next: what if they bought an owner-occupant property with 5% down, then bought up to nine more rental properties, each with 20% down payments and invested the rest in stocks?

With static assumptions that's about 3.5 years faster than just renting and buying ten 20% down payment rentals:

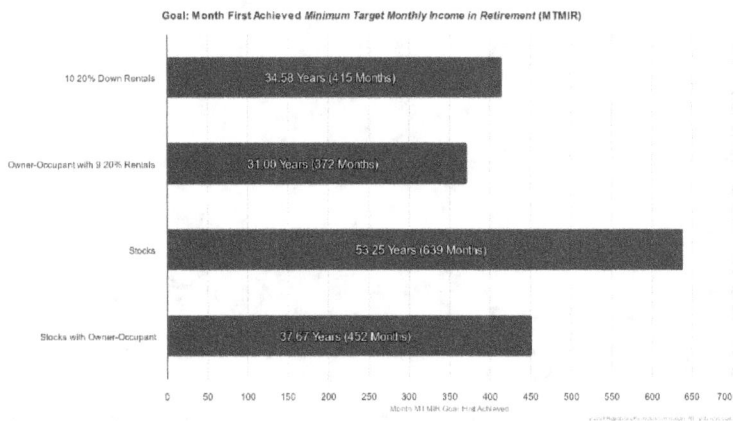

Goal: Month First Achieved *Minimum Target Monthly Income in Retirement (MTMIR)*

If we do Monte Carlo modeling, it looks like this:

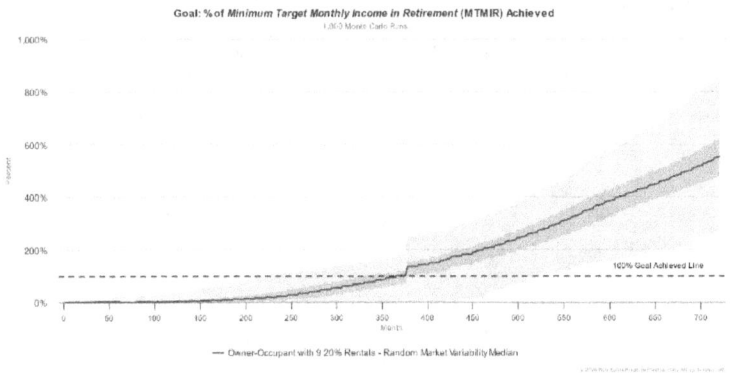

Doing a very busy version of this chart by comparing it to the other strategies so far, it looks like this:

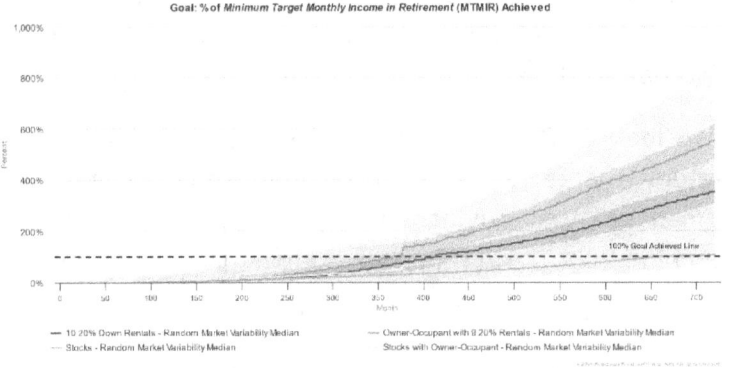

130

If we just look at the 50th percentile (median) value for the four options:

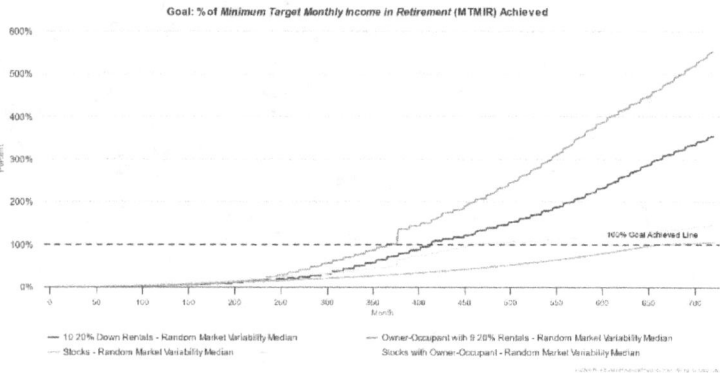

It shows that buying the owner-occupant property and nine 20% down payment rentals appears to be faster and gives them a higher standard of living than even buying ten 20% down payment rentals.

If we look at the percentage of the 1,000 runs for reach strategy that achieved financial independence and when, we can see that buying an owner-occupant property and then nine 20% down rentals is the best performer yet:

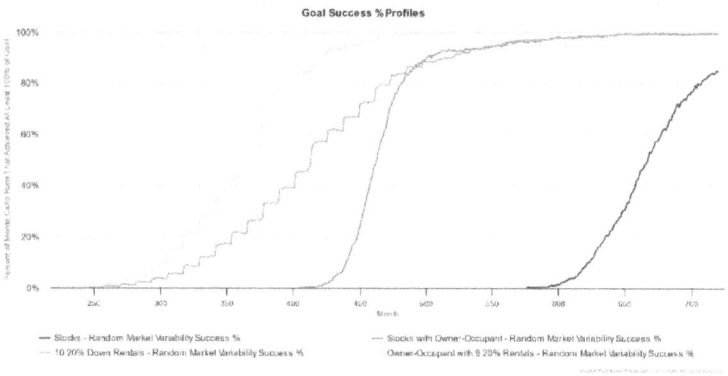

In the chart above you can see that not only does financial independence tend to happen faster (a little to the left on the chart), it also tends to be more consistent (a higher percentage of the runs achieve FI).

Nomad™ Real Estate Investing Strategy Example

There's so much more we could do with this, but for now I'll wrap it up with a slight curve ball.

Instead of buying an owner-occupant property and then buying nine 20% down payment rentals, let's imagine they Nomad™.

- They buy an owner-occupant property with 5% down payment.
- They live there for *at least* a year. That's a requirement of the lender to get an owner-occupant loan with an owner-occupant down payment and owner-occupant mortgage interest rate.
- Once their year is up AND they've saved up enough for another 5% down payment, they buy another owner-occupant property and move into it.
- They take the previous property they were living in and convert it to a rental property
- They repeat this until they have 9 rentals and the property they're living in

Instead of having to save up for 20% down payments, they acquire the same nine rental properties with only 5% down on each by moving into each one as an owner-occupant.

Is this better? Is this more probable for them to be financially independent? Is this faster to financial independence? Does this give a higher standard of living than the other strategies so far? And—we won't cover it here because it is a longer discussion—but is it more or less risky?

It turns out that with static assumptions (not Monte Carlo modeling yet), Nomad™ is 58 months (almost 5 years) faster to financial independence.

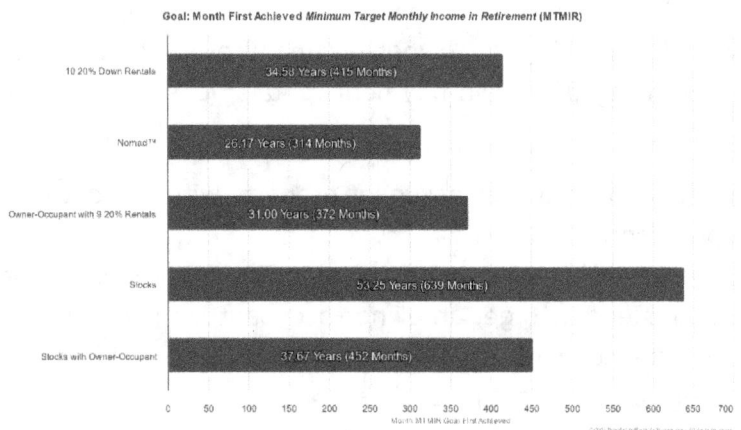

Goal: Month First Achieved *Minimum Target Monthly Income in Retirement (MTMIR)*

If we add variability and do Monte Carlo modeling, we can look at how the Nomad™ strategy performs in the chart below:

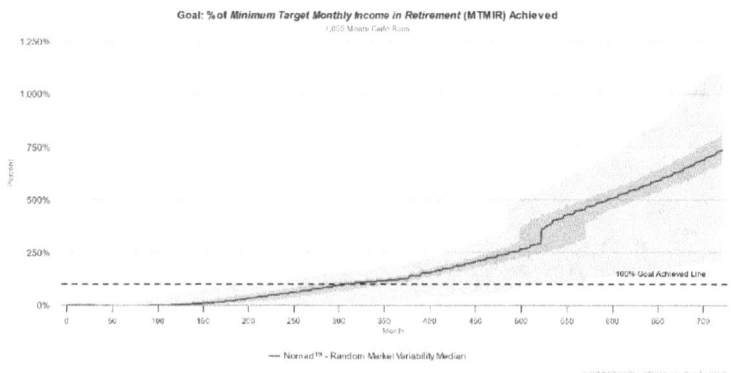

Brace yourself for the busy version comparing them all at the same time:

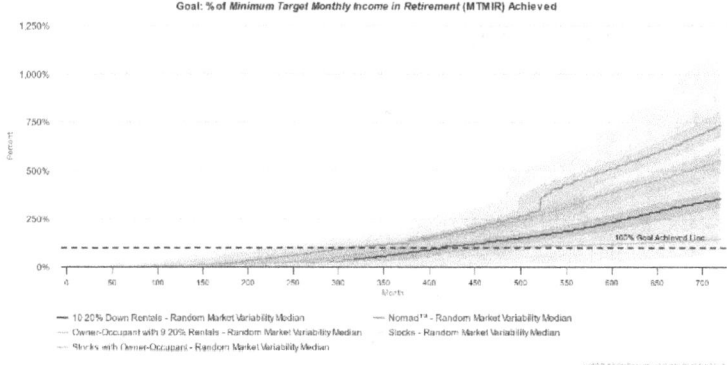

And, if we turn off the range of results and just look at the middle most (median) of the 1,000 runs for each strategy, we can see the following:

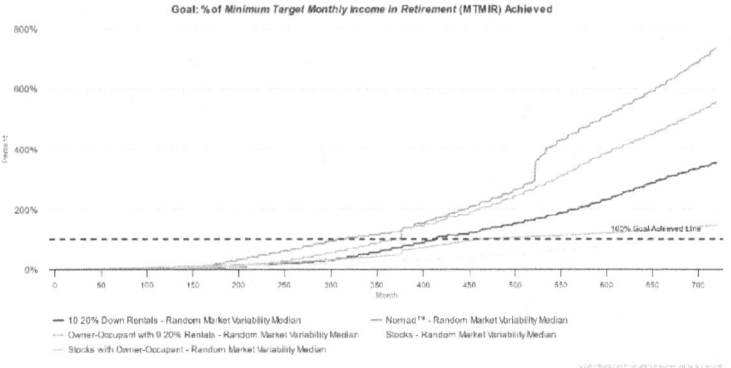

Goal: % of Minimum Target Monthly Income in Retirement (MTMIR) Achieved

Still a bit busy to see what is going on, but I will point out, in the chart above, the Nomad™ strategy seems to give them the fastest achievement of financial independence and highest standard of living.

Isn't it interesting.

If we look at the percentage of the 1,000 runs that achieve financial independence and by when you can see even better:

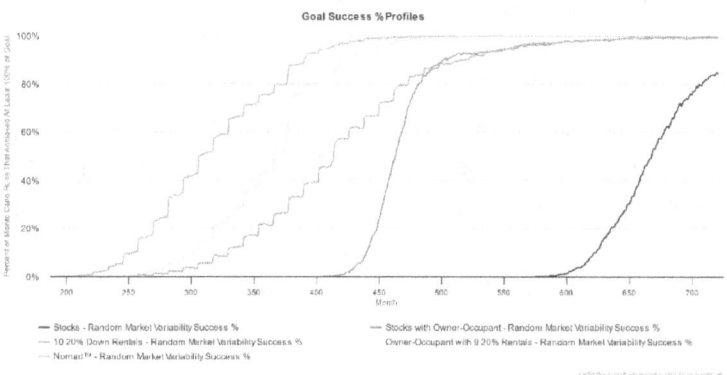

The Nomad™ strategy achieves financial independence earliest (to the left on the chart above). It also has a higher probability of being financially independent earlier.

Additional Modeling

Now that we know the importance of considering the variability that might occur in the future, this is really just the beginning.

There is a ridiculous amount more to dig into here. We've just barely scratched the surface.

There's a lot more to model.

For example, we could model each strategy you're considering seeing how each strategy performs:

136

- Buying long-term buy and hold rental properties (short-term rentals, medium-term rentals, student rentals, storage units, assisted living, apartments, etc)
- Buying properties utilizing creative financing (owner financing, wrap financing, loan assumptions, rent-to-owns, agreements for deed, subject-to)
- Variations on the Nomad™ strategy (Nomad™ by Proxy, Nomad™ with House Hacking, Nomad™ to Short-Term Rental, Nomad™ with Lease-Option Exits, *The Ultimate Real Estate Agent Retirement Plan*™)
- House Hacking and related strategies
- Short-Term Rentals and related strategies
- Flipping properties and related strategies
- BRRRR and related strategies
- And much, much more

Or, combining one or more of these strategies at the same time (fix and flipping while acquiring long-term or short-term rentals as an example) or sequentially (fix and flipping for 10 years then switch to buy and hold).

Or, we could test a wide assortment of variations to your strategy:

- More or less reserves (and its impact on both speed and risk)
- More or less down payment size up to buying properties for all cash
- Buying down interest rates or not
- Getting roommates or not (house hacking)
- Selling via lease-options versus with a real estate agent or for sale by owner

- Paying off properties early with extra cash flow versus not
- Doing cash out refinances to buy additional properties faster
- Buying properties and selling them when you could take the proceeds (after all expenses including taxes) and then investing that money in stocks, bonds or something else to be financially independent
- Buying more properties than you need and selling them to pay off properties when it means you'd be financially independent
- And much, much more

Not Just Financial Independence

When we do these models, it is important to consider more than just how fast you're able to get to financial independence—even though that's what we focused on here.

Sometimes it is about your standard of living once you are financially independent. Some strategies might just barely get you to your minimum required income to be financially independent. While others will give you far more each month than you initially stated you needed allowing you to live at a much higher standard of living than you originally required.

Sometimes, it is about measuring, comparing and ultimately minimizing risks. Some strategies are riskier than others. They might get you to financial independence, on average, 1 year faster, but there's a 20 times greater chance you'll run out of money by pursuing that strategy than another one that gets you to financial independence, on average, a year slower.

That all might be worth considering... especially for your own unique situation.

It is important for you to evaluate your own strategy utilizing Monte Carlo modeling to better understand how to achieve financial independence faster, easier, with higher probability of success, with a higher standard of living and with less overall risk.

Or, if you are going to ignore one or more of those things, deliberately and strategically choosing to ignore them with full knowledge of the consequences.

About the Author

James Orr is a seasoned real estate investor and the visionary creator of the Real Estate Financial Planner™ software. With a passion for sharing his wealth of knowledge, James has authored numerous books on real estate investing, covering a wide array of topics to help both novice and experienced investors succeed.

Living in Loveland, Colorado, James enjoys a fulfilling life with his wife, Tammy, whom he has been happily married to since 1995. Together, they have raised two grown sons. When he's not writing or managing his real estate investments, James is dedicated to teaching others the secrets of financial independence through smart property investments.

Also by James Orr

- The Real Estate Investing Mentor series of topic books
- How to Achieve Financial Independence and Live Your Passion Regardless of Age or Income: 10 Paths to Financial Independence Analyzed
- How to Acquire a Multi-Million Dollar Real Estate Portfolio With Just $3,000
- How to Acquire a Multi-Million Dollar Real Estate Portfolio Earning Just $5,000 Per Month
- Nomad™
- Ultimate Nomad™ Checklist
- Northern Colorado Real Estate Advisor
- Acquiring a Portfolio of Cash Flowing Properties In Northern Colorado: A Real Estate Financial Planner™ Blueprint
- Real Estate Investing Systems

Software and Spreadsheets

- Real Estate Financial Planner™ software
- The World's Greatest Real Estate Deal Analysis Spreadsheet™
- Should I Sell My Rental Property Spreadsheet™
- Should I Refinance My Rental Property Spreadsheet™
- CapEx Estimator for Rental Property – Basic and Advanced Spreadsheets
- Financial Independence Asset Allocation and Cash Flow Engines Spreadsheet™
- The Investor's Agent One-Page Business Plan™

A Small Request

Thank you for reading *The Real Estate Investing Mentor: The Affordable $50K Coaching Alternative* topic book on **Should I Refinance My Rental Property?**

I am positive if you follow what I've written, you will be on your way to successfully investing in real estate. When you do please reach out and share your story.

I have a small, quick favor to ask. Would you mind taking a minute or two and leaving an honest review for this book on Amazon?

Reviews are the BEST way to help others purchase this book and keep the price of my books low for everyone, and I check all my reviews looking for helpful feedback.

Please visit:

https://REFP.info/should-i-refi-book

Questions?

Thank you for taking the time to read this book. If a concept sparked a question or if you feel there's an area that could be explained more clearly, I'd truly appreciate hearing from you. You can reach me at **jamesorr@gmail.com** with any feedback specific to this title. My goal is to make each book as helpful and practical as possible, and your input plays a big part in that.

Just a note—while I'm here to help deepen your understanding of this book's topics, this isn't intended as a personal coaching service. For advice tailored to your own situation, I encourage you to work closely with a real estate agent who can provide the insight and support unique to your goals.

Thank you again for reading, and for helping me make this series an even better resource for investors like you.

www.ingramcontent.com/pod-product-compliance
Lightning Source LLC
Chambersburg PA
CBHW071504220526
45472CB00003B/910